PENGUIN BOOKS

SPEAK SUNLIGHT

Alan Jolis is the author of the acclaimed novel *Mercedes and the House of Rainbows*. He was born in New York in 1953 and now lives in Paris. His children's novel, *The Last Laugh*, has been shortlisted for two French literary awards, Prix du Meilleur Premier Roman pour Enfants and Prix des Incorruptibles. His new novel, *Fouche's Last Night*, is a detective story set during the French Revolution and has been optioned for a film production.

SPEAK SUNLIGHT

A MEMOIR

Alan Jolis

PENGUIN BOOKS

For my giant of a father, Albert Jolis,
and for his smallest grandson, Jeremy Albert

My eternal gratitude to
Rosalie Siegel and Leslie Gardner,
my literary agents, whose professionalism,
dedication and loyalty have no limits

PENGUIN BOOKS

Published by the Penguin Group
Penguin Books Ltd, 27 Wrights Lane, London W8 5TZ, England
Penguin Books USA Inc., 375 Hudson Street, New York, New York 10014, USA
Penguin Books Australia Ltd, Ringwood, Victoria, Australia
Penguin Books Canada Ltd, 10 Alcorn Avenue, Toronto, Ontario, Canada M4V 3B2
Penguin Books (NZ) Ltd, 182–190 Wairau Road, Auckland 10, New Zealand

Penguin Books Ltd, Registered Offices: Harmondsworth, Middlesex, England

First published by Hamish Hamilton 1996
Published in Penguin Books 1997
1 3 5 7 9 10 8 6 4 2

Printed in England by Clays Ltd, St Ives plc

Anti-Foreword

Gustave Flaubert at the death of his mistress wrote, 'I have stepped on so many things in order to be able to live.' I too find myself standing on the shoulders of my loved ones, and *Speak Sunlight* is written not so much for them as with them, my progenitors. I never said goodbye to any of these people properly, and because I will never be able to repay them I dedicated my first novel to them.

In this book I use their real names, so it is indeed strange that I do not use my own. I tried – I wrote a draft in which I called the narrator Alanito. But while this was literally true, it felt less emotionally truthful: an invented name gave me more freedom and more truth. I can't explain why this is. Yet, intimate and naked as I feel when I reread *Speak Sunlight*, at times it seems as if I am looking at my youth through the wrong end of a telescope, and if this were in any sense an autobiography I would have much more to say, more details to describe. If pressed to give the book a label, I would call it a love song.

No matter how far afield I may go, *Speak Sunlight* will always bring me back to something essential. This is my truth, as distilled as I can make it. The important thing is not whether any small part of this may be fabrication, but how large a place these events occupy in my soul, and how much they haunt me.   *Alan Jolis*

'¡Basta!' dijo la marquesa,
y puso sus dos tetas encima de la mesa.
(Manolo wit)

CHAPTER ONE
Maruja

I remember her round face constantly bursting into laughter. Her pudgy cheeks, double chin, have no age. She is such a fireball of energy and humour that most people don't even ask her age, and even though a glandular condition renders her almost as wide as she is tall they overlook her unfortunate shape. She defies labels, defies ready-made descriptions. In my memory, she is *sui generis*. She just is there – leaping into my life as if she had always belonged in it, always controlled it.

I see her rushing on little chubby legs to the market, dragging back a two-wheeled food-cart. She could be twenty-five, or maybe closer to forty.

I remember her mostly smiling over a hot stove, working in a kitchen two and a half by three and a half metres which most people would not use as a closet. And in that bath of steam, that cloud of sizzling olive oil, in a frenzy of orders and counter-orders, jokes, invocations for the Blessed Mary to give her patience with me, prayers to Joseph, self-deprecations, screams, laughter, half in French,

I

half in her native Gallego, I see her spoonfeeding me: 'Eat, *niño*, eat. You are as skinny as a bird.'

It is in that tiny space that she prepares sumptuous dishes for my parents' dinner parties: *poularde au riz sauce suprème, osso buco trovatore, canard aux olives, turbot en croûte avec béchamel, riz de veau, raie au beurre noir* – the dishes go singing out of that greasy yellow kitchen as if confected in a five-star restaurant by a world-class chef. They go out on silver trays carried over one shoulder by her husband. With Manolo's dignified long face to serve them, the dishes take on a nobility and upper-class panache totally incongruous with the hell and noise of the small kitchen.

I see myself running down the long hallway to the vestibule where I can watch Manolo serving the meal as if he were the Prince of the Long Countenance. His black dress shoes curl up at the edges due to his corns. His dress pants have a tendency to slip down his thin waistline, past his hips, but the gold-buttoned jacket ironed to perfection rehabilitates all that his lower regions leave to be desired.

I spy on the guests. In the full-length antique mirrors that line the dining-room, the faces and names melt into an upper-class jet-set of donkey-braying laughs. The meal runs on as smoothly as a rip in a silk stocking. But they see only the surface of things – they ignore the hours of preparation, the battleground disaster that is Maruja's little bastion of sanity. Now and then they comment on the food and ask Manolo to congratulate the chef. He nods shyly and moves on, serving the next guest from the left, bending at the waist, holding the wide serving dish perfectly still. Someone asks him for the secret of Maruja's *turbot en béchamel*. The entire table stops and looks at him as steam from the sauce-covered white fish rises into his face and curls around his cheeks. Manolo turns red.

On duty he never smiles, but he serves with the delicacy and tension of an actor who has done long battle with stage fright. His black hair is thick, almost negroid, with tiny grey filaments at the temples. No comb can survive being pulled through such crêpe-like hair, but every day he works and reworks it for almost twenty minutes, expertly slipping the thin handle of a brush under the layers of hair and pushing the whole affair up, giving it greater height and body.

I run back to Maruja and recount to her the praise that is being heaped on her. She pretends not to care, but the already frenetic energy level around her stove goes up one octave. She is alive and happy, sweat pouring off her carmine face. Maruja rules the rear quarters of the house with a mixture of lavish screaming and banging of pots, barely stopping to throw old dishes into the overflowing sink.

'They weren't six, they were twelve! No no no no, one day your sainted mother, may God forgive her thoughtlessness, will kill me. I swear it cannot go on like this. She invites people she doesn't even know. I can't. I refuse!'

Maruja is used to my mother's American over-generosity

by now; she too has that same love of the spontaneous and the anarchic, but last-minute additional guests always put her meals into an orbit of hyper-agitation.

'This is not a house, it's a hotel!'

By the time the guests leave, Maruja is slumped in a straight-backed white wooden chair, smoking one of her filter Cool menthol cigarettes, hoarse and staring with glazed eyes at the pile of dirty dishes.

My bedroom, and right next to it Maruja and Manolo's room, and the kitchen constitute a world on its own, overlooking the inner courtyard, seldom visited by my father. But tonight the long slow metronome beat of his footsteps announces that he is on his way down the long hallway.

'Manola? You there?'

French and English speakers call her 'Manola' because they cannot pronounce the rolled 'r' or the guttural 'hhha' of 'Maruja'. He speaks to her in French, for his Spanish is quite rusty.

'*Sí, monsieur?*'

'It was excellent, Manola. But next time my wife invites more people without any warning, I want you simply to refuse.'

He stands in the kitchen like an admiral of the fleet not noticing that the engine-room is in any way too small, or unsuited for the work demanded of it. With a definite *noblesse oblige*, he ignores the stains on the floor and the grease on the walls. Standing by the sink, wiping her face,

4

Maruja smiles. Whenever he sets foot back here, her many complaints disappear.

'Yes, you must refuse!'

'*No, no, no es nada, señor.*' Being my mother's soulmate, Maruja cannot do anything but defend her madness.

'You are too good with *madame*, too generous, Manola. She will never learn if you let her get away with this.'

My father is a model of tradition, a man born with a silver spoon in his mouth, and while she respects him and worships him as a stand-in for the father she never had, they meet so seldom and in such restricted conditions that their discussions only serve to emphasize the gulf that separates them.

Maruja and my mother are total opposites. Everything separates them – education, taste, social position, culture. Maruja always calls her *señora* and uses the formal *usted*, yet she advises her on her marriage, her sons, everything. Maruja is not so much a loyal sister as one of those maids in Molière comedies who are smarter than their masters, and who conspire to make things turn out all right in the end. She tells her things even her best friends don't dare tell her. She tells her, '*Señora*, pay more attention to your husband, or you will lose him, *madame*.' And of course, she is prescient in this as in most other things. Often one can find them seated at the kitchen table like sisters.

With Maruja in the house, there are no longer the periodic personality clashes that always in the past ended in slamming doors and tears, and in the cook leaving. She is with us to stay, part of the family, and the fact that I spend most of my vacations with her is perfectly natural.

Since they arrived, Maruja and Manolo let me crawl into their bed on Saturday and Sunday mornings. It is the warmest, kindest, smelliest bed I know.

Maruja is from a dirt-poor backwater of Galicia, on Spain's north-west coast. Her father, an alcoholic, abandoned the family when she was a baby, and her mother died shortly thereafter of heartbreak. The youngest of five daughters, she was raised by her eldest sister. She grew up never wearing shoes and learned to beg from American navymen whose ships anchored in Vigo. 'Gimme chewing-gum, mister' were the only words of English she knew.

Her sisters became farmers, but Maruja had an energy, vivacity and charm wholly superior to anyone in her village. She came to Paris and in spite of not speaking a word of French she got a job cooking for an elderly French count. The day the count hired Manolo, the tall impeccably dressed Basque, as his butler, Maruja fell into such a panic that she burned the lunch. It was love at first sight, at least for her.

The short Gallego peasant and the aristocratic urbane Basque make, they say, a perfect couple. She thinks and laughs enough for both of them, she makes all the decisions.

I am certain she talked him into marrying her.

Their bedroom is right behind mine; in fact we share

one wall so I can hear their marital discord and bickering coming at me muted and fuzzy. This whole evening they scream at each other, each threatening to pack their suitcase and walk out of this marriage. It seems to me impossible that Maruja and Manolo fight so bitterly and still make a life together. Unable to sleep, I listen to their shouts and the slamming of doors. When they first moved in I was terrified of these episodic outbursts, then I tried to ignore them, now I am almost bored with them. Above all I would like them to argue in their own time and let me sleep.

Manolo rushes into my room and updates me on their argument. I am an active participant in their quarrel, giving Manolo opinions he has not asked for and new arguments. It is not that I want to betray Maruja – if she ran in asking for advice, I would no doubt take her side just as readily – but Manolo is so shy, so henpecked, so in need of help.

Now he sits on the edge of my bed and whispers all the terrible things she has said to him tonight.

'*Es una loca, una loca perdida*,' I keep telling him, trying to buck him up, giving him whatever all-male assistance I can.

'Pack your bags and go, Manolo. Leave her.'

'Yes, that is exactly what I am going to do.'

'But don't just threaten it like you always do, this time do it. She doesn't believe you any more.'

'Yes, this time I am leaving. That is for certain.'

7

I sit up in bed and wait while he goes in to Maruja. For a while I wonder if he is actually packing his bags. I feel guilty. Have I helped break up their marriage? I don't want them divorced at all, but it seems the only way to end this endless argument, to get them each out of this rut.

Manolo comes back, breathless. 'Now she is having one of her attacks,' he says, and listens to the silence.

I stare at his square chin, the white skin just hanging loose. He smells of aftershave. He has a soft voice. Some hairs in his neck are unshaved. I stare at the buttons of his shirt, which he has methodically and painstakingly buttoned. I have seen Manolo tie and retie his triangular V-shaped knot ten times, until it fills up his collar and he gets the tie lengths just right. For days on end, he removes it by running the knot and leaving the tie made so he can just slip it over his head in the morning already done. His hands smell of soap.

'Is it a real attack?'

'I don't know.'

He will never leave her — he can't survive without her, or maybe he can, but from years of Maruja telling him that he can't, that she is his courage, his brains and his soul, he has started believing it. And maybe she is right.

'Don't give in to her blackmail, Manolo.'

I can tell he is barely listening; then he asks me, 'Why do people get married and live through such *mierda*?' We both wait. I feel he is trapped; I am trapped too, in a web that will never let us go. We can hear Maruja sobbing next door. He goes to her. I listen to their voices rise and fall, the whispers speed up and then slow down.

There is a crash like someone's head slamming on to the floor, and then nothing. Silence. I wait for Manolo to come and report, but he doesn't. Nothing.

I get out of bed and go look for myself. My parents have no idea what goes on back at our end of the apartment.

I find Maruja lying across her bed, head thrown back, eyes rolling back into her head, moaning. For years I have heard about her *ataques de nervios*, but I've never actually seen one. Now I am terrified. Why are the doctors unable to diagnose her ailment? Foam is forming at the corners of her mouth. Lying unconscious, her body writhes from side to side. I don't dare say a thing. Is she possessed? Is this epilepsy?

'It's her nerves,' says Manolo, seated at her side, looking bored but also embarrassed as if he wishes she would snap out of it. Her hand lies inert in his. Now and then she sighs.

'Is she going to die?'

'No, this is a small attack.'

She claims these attacks come upon her when she least expects it, but somehow I assume they are slightly choreographed for maximum effect.

'What did you do to her, Manolo?'

'Nothing.'

The attacks generally last a couple of hours, and she feels

tired but better the next morning. Her body continues in a trance, I watch her convulse on the bed from side to side. I can't stand this. The foam at her lips is freaking me out, and also the way her eyeballs roll back into her head.

I am glad I am not in Manolo's shoes.

'Is she going to die?'

Manolo calls a doctor. For once my mother is not paying the cook under the table, and that means social security will cover her.

Breakfast in the kitchen is just me and her. And Radio France on her small transistor plugged into the wall. Sunlight is pouring down through the narrow window. I am seated at the small rectangular table with a rough red-checked tablecloth. Not a word is said about last night. Maruja is in a good mood again, and I don't want to dispel it.

An odd rumbling stops us. Maruja looks inside the stove, laughing that the ghost of some duck she cooked yesterday has come back to haunt her. She discovers that a baby pigeon has fallen out of its nest on to the window-sill. She brings him in and feeds him milk. The baby acquires a big white metal cage and becomes a staple of the kitchen. ('One thing has to change here,' she says, 'for everything to stay the same.') All summer long that bird lives sumptuously between the kitchen window and the sink. In the fall when he is big and strong, Maruja and I give him back his freedom.

★

Every night my father sits in his favourite armchair, and I recount to him what I ate at lunch at the school cafeteria.

He who was starved as an English public schoolboy listens with amazement as I describe *boudin noir, canard à l'orange, côtes de porc aux prunes, sole meunière.* I can see in his eyes at least a restaurant atmosphere with someone like Manolo bending to serve us, so I don't disillusion him, I do not mention the pats of butter we send ceilingward, the spoon attacks, the elbow wars, the stainless steel serving dishes so bruised they can't stay put on the table but keep seesawing as if they wanted to hop back into the kitchen.

I am the only one of her four sons who has ever been able to demand the attention of her husband, and my mother admires this performance. My father, who is now fifty, lets me get away with things he would never have tolerated from my older brothers. They were expected to remain out of sight and simply play in their room, back by the maid's quarters, but I actually trundle out to his armchair in the living-room every school evening, interrupt his nightly newspaper and recite my lunch litany. This has become a ritual for us, and I imagine that in a way he even looks forward to my speech concerning my little day.

Well, in that same way my mother now wants me to ask my father officially if I may be allowed to go with Maruja to Spain for my summer vacation. It surprises me that I have to go through this charade, this test by fire when it could all be decided behind my back by the adults. I have been on two summer vacations with Maruja already, why must I keep on presenting a formal request? Everyone in the house knows I am going with them for the summer, how can my father not know?

But Maruja also insists I get his blessing.

'If I am going to be responsible for you, it has to be established formally with your father.'

OK, so we go, she and I, sheepish down the long corridor. I in my bathrobe and slippers, showered, and ready for bed. She has smoked her one Cool a night; her black hair is combed back in bouffant leonine fashion, so her high forehead and round face stand out for all to admire. In her black uniform, she is excited at the prospect of facing my father in the living-room.

He is enjoying his after-dinner whisky, which lends his cheek and his clothes a scent far sharper and more memorable to me (Vat 69, Black & White, Ballantine's, J & B) than my mother's perfumes. I stand before him self-conscious, as he studies the editorial page. My father is so particular about the crease in his newspaper that no one dares read it before him, and all day it sits folded in the entrance hall waiting for his fingers. My mother announces that I have something to say. Maruja is off to one side, so he must know what I am going to say, but he waits patiently.

'Dad, can I go to Spain with Maruja this summer?'

'Is that what you want to do?'

'Yes.'

It never crosses my mind to go on any vacation with

him; he is an international businessman, always working, always on the phone or flying off to some meeting.

Maruja smiles broadly, for she adores the orderly Chairman of the Board approach he brings to bear on all decisions. There is nothing Maruja enjoys quite as much as stiff-upper-lip British formality — everything that she is not.

My father smiles at her as if he were the last man on earth who should be making this decision. 'You really want him on your holiday, Manola?'

'*Sí, señor.*'

'Well, it won't be too peaceful!'

To be polite, she joins him in laughter.

CHAPTER TWO

Irún–Hendaye

In our second-class compartment, I stare at the dirty head-rests wondering when was the last year these were sent to the dry-cleaner. The smell of peeled oranges coats the air. Maruja sits forward, staring through the grimy gummed-up windows at the passing countryside. All passengers are required to get out at the border, but still she sits like someone intent on not missing her stop. I notice her wipe her face with the flat of her hand. The tears that avoid her fingers bloom on the collar of her white blouse. A long stream of water is slipping down her cheeks.

'I can't help it, *niño*.' She taps her chest and tries laughing. 'The smell of my country explodes in my heart.'

During the long wet winters in Paris, she never voices homesickness or desire for sunshine, but as soon as she approaches Irún, she is like a teenager preparing for her first date.

I see us dragging suitcases. We look like chain-gang workers each dragging our ball and chain behind us. Every ten feet I stop and breathe.

'What did you pack, Maruja, pavement stones?'

'Be quiet, and hurry up!'

Maruja's French has never progressed beyond the food-ordering stage, so we always speak Spanish together.

Her supposedly leather bags are made of a material which over the years has become as soft and thin as old cardboard, but perhaps they always were cardboard, which is why Maruja ties strong ropes around them.

'Come on, *niño*, hurry up, quickly! *Veeeennnnn, niño!*'

Today's level of hollering and sweating is unusual even by Maruja's generous standards. Manolo is not with us (he will join us in a fortnight), so she cannot heap abuse on him.

The original suitcase handles, mended at Prisunic, broke off somewhere in the Gare d'Austerlitz, and now my aching hands are cut raw from the ropes.

We dash past the haughty, dismissive French customs officials, down into an underpass. We have an impossible connection to make, and so we scramble, dragging our suitcases.

'Why can't France and Spain agree on the width of their train tracks?'

'So Napoleon can invade us again?' Maruja is serious.

In the large Irún customs hall, I struggle to get our suitcases to lie flat for the inspectors.

The *carabinero*, a man with a piece of white chalk in his fingers and a curt thin moustache, approaches. He doesn't lower himself to fiddling with our suitcases but stands there angry. Dignity in France is demonstrated by scowling and acting as if someone just kicked you up the ass. And this Spanish border official has watched too many Frenchmen: he is mad at his job, angry at us for standing in front of him, angry at the piece of chalk for being in his fingers.

Maruja, a *macha* through and through, borrows a pocket-knife and cuts the rope for him. She does that to protect the next suitcase, which contains the coffee, chocolate and tea she is bringing in illegally.

Last year, a gentleman who passed through our train compartment asked if we had any coffee. And, thinking he wanted to borrow some, I answered, 'Oh yes, of course, we have coffee.' Since then Maruja has explained to me the importance of silence, and this year I am wiser and far quieter.

The *carabinero* wants to see the other suitcase. He peers in as Maruja unfolds her dresses, her bras as big as a catcher's mitt. Her expert fingers sift everything without any coffee or chocolate tumbling out. The man holds the chalk as if it were a cancer eating his fingers, and with an expression of disgust mixed with contempt draws a barely-visible X on the suitcase.

Lowly travellers, we hoist our suitcases full of misery and dash towards freedom.

For a moment, I imagine an Olympic event – The Irún five-hundred-metre death-scramble, in which all the contestants would carry anvils in their suitcases, and the judges would misinform them about the train schedules and platforms, and the station would be an obstacle course of backpackers and sleeping no-counts. No one, of course, would ever find out who the winner is.

I trip and knock to a halt in front of an electric board, where Maruja is searching for a train conductor or a station master. Suddenly she sits down on her suitcase and points to a blue Talgo express leaving the station.

'Well, we're on vacation now, what do we care?'

'Was that it?'

'*Sí!*'

Maruja laughs, noticing that on the last two-hundred-metre dash the heel broke off her left shoe. She takes this opportunity to massage the soles of her feet, which today have swelled into red balloons. It never ceases to amaze me that any shoe could carry her weight day in and day out.

I kick and cajole my suitcase towards the toilet. Peeing, I ignore the ill-breathing, sweaty old men who wheeze and spit into the butt-filled urinals.

Back in the station, I can't see Maruja. Panic sets in. Just a second ago she had stopped to palaver, a veiled excuse to slip her feet out of her shoes and to uncrease her wounded hands, but now she has vanished! Without Maruja, it dawns on me how unsuited I am for this Irún subworld. I speak Spanish, but the gold teeth, the mouths purple from wine, the peasants sleeping on the ground, none of this inspires confidence. I smile at strangers but pray to God they don't approach me or touch me. Even the RENFE train conductors with their timetables and their silver whistles don't look trustworthy. I am Lord Fauntleroy, the crown prince, abandoned in a leper colony.

Searching for Maruja, I become aware, as never before, that Spain is still a police state. It is 1961; few here discuss the civil war, but my parents, both supporters of the Republic, invited countless Spanish *émigrés* for dinner, heroic Basque secessionists like Lezo, and anti-fascist freedom fighters like Julián Gorkin and his sister the ballet dancer Lolita, and for as long as I can remember I heard of their exploits. Suddenly all those horror stories are spinning in my head. A cartoon by Bartoli, the Catalan artist, hangs in my room; it shows a body in the distance, and up close a *Guardia Civil* with his gun still smoking. It's entitled, simply, *La Muerte*. I see that same *Muerte* stalking the train platforms here in Irún.

Maruja wipes her face and mutters, '*Bendito sea Dios, que ese maldito tren este donde usted diga, señor.*'

I rush to her side. I've never been so happy to spy her butterball figure before.

The train conductor she is talking to is joined by two *Guardias Civiles*, tall and handsome in their shiny patent-leather tri-cornered hats (which they wear with no sense of ridicule at all). They ignore this Calcutta atmosphere, the bundles, the flies, the bodies of stranded travellers wrapped in blankets and sprawled out on the cement floors, and fix their eyes on the horizon. Irún's cocktail of soldiers, border guards, undercover security, customs officials and élite anti-contrabandists is here not to provide assistance but to give the pathetic rabble a sense of the dignity that is Franco's Spain.

Maruja thanks the conductor, and we clatter down the steps of the train underpass. Her broken black shoes clack-clack on each cement step, a staccato accompaniment to the deep-throated thuds of her bouncing suitcase. Even though her right elbow is hoisted up as far as it will go, the suitcase never clears the ground. I follow. It seems to me that only women and children are lugging rocks around the Irún station. The men are smoking, watching, or dozing on benches and ignoring their wives and families as best they can. It would never cross their minds to lend us a hand; it would not be *macho*.

Maruja stands in line to change money. The thick wad of Spanish bills she receives in return barely fits into her billfold. 'Let's go eat *churros*! We have time now.'

We leave our suitcases next to an old woman who, wrapped in a black shawl, appears to be sleeping with her eyes open.

'Would you be so kind as to watch over our bags, *señora*,' Maruja asks. The notion that anyone could possibly run off with our suitcases is laughable, but I am too tired to argue. Anyway, I have to keep up with Maruja because with only her black pocketbook to carry, she moves fast. Through a forest of legs I keep a firm eye on those chubby calves of hers.

I find her with one elbow on the small *churros* stand,

smiling. '*Mira, mira, niño*, this is how they make the *churros*!'

Maruja by herself is far more spontaneous than with Manolo. He worries about what people might think or say (the famous *qué dirán?*), but Maruja has no such bourgeois qualms. Since crossing the border, her voice has grown thirty per cent louder, more self-assured. She is all smiles now.

'Two orders of *churros*, please.'

Little has changed here since the Civil War. All manner of cripples and gypsies try to bum a cigarette, or sell us tombola tickets. And Maruja's insistence that we dress our best for the trip ('What if they have to rush you to the hospital?') makes us stand out as the *crème de la crème* of the *churros* stand. Even her excess corpulence does not catch the *churros* man's attention. He looks at her, in her blue and white polka-dot *tailleur*, as if she were a lady of taste and refinement; her weight is a detail of no significance. Nothing servant-like about her.

While the *churros* man squeezes out a continuous concentric filament of batter into a pan full of sizzling olive oil, Maruja turns her face to the morning sun and closes her eyes. She smiles as round as a sunflower. I watch the beige serpent in the pan turn dark. The *churros* man pulls it out of the boiling oil, crispy and thick, and, holding it with tongs, snips it with scissors. Grease soaks through the paper napkin on the plate and through the powdered sugar he sprinkles on top.

'It's hot, *señora*, be careful.'

Maruja dunks the steaming end of a *churro* into her hot cocoa and uses a square single-ply waxy paper napkin to wipe her lips.

'*Aie aie aie.*' She sways, opening her mouth and blowing out to cool her tongue. '*Te gusta, niño?*'

'*Sí,*' I lie.

The chocolate is so sweet my teeth ache. The best part of this *churros* ritual is the tall glass of water.

'No, he is not mine,' she tells the *churros* man, admiring my haircut and straightening my collar. She uses her fingers to brush sugar sprinkles off my cheeks. 'He belongs to my *señora*.'

Maruja can't have children, and that is why she likes to holler in public to me, *niño* this and *niño* that. I give her the impression that she has a child. It is a conceit that I know helps us here because in Spain a woman with a child in tow can do no wrong.

She flashes that look I have gotten to know well, a look of wanting to smother me in kisses.

'He is almost my own. This *niño* is more mine than he is his mother's. I have had him since he was four. I take him everywhere. He sleeps in my bed, eats my food. I dress him, wash him, snot him. I take him to church.'

Her lips curl up with each of my bites as if to help me eat. I could spill all the *churros*, spill my chocolate, I could piss and shit myself and her screaming would only be a lure to make others think she was doing her job disciplining me. But I have never known her anger to be real.

'I can't, Maruja.'

'*Niño, por favor*. Don't make me finish them, you'll make me blow up like a balloon.'

'Go ahead, eat them, Maruja!'

She nods to the *churros* salesman, indicating to him that her size is my fault.

'*Niño*, look, this dress has become too tight for me.'

'It's fine.'

'You will kill me.'

Keeping track of imperceptible weight changes is a snobbism, a pretence of sounding semi-French acquired since she and my mother started going on diets together, but Maruja's weight bears no relation to how much or how little she eats.

She pays for the *churros* with regal abandon.

Most of the way south is through tunnels and along arid rocky ridges, but in our compartment, which smells of old socks and peeled oranges, Maruja keeps staring out at the countryside and smiling. She sits hands on her knees and partakes of her one guilty pleasure, a menthol Cool. She blows out the smoke without inhaling and is blessedly quiet for a while.

Coffee is the one staple her doctors tell her to avoid on account of her nerves. When the soft-drink man makes it over the barrage of suitcases in the passageway, she explains to him how bad Spanish coffee is: 'Just glorified wood chips and chicory compared to American coffee, but OK, give me two cups.'

CHAPTER THREE

Pamplona la Vieja

For all the factories and tall smokestacks that surround it, Pamplona still looks like a medieval fortified city built on a hill with machicolated walls and imposing city gates.

The *peseta* is cheap and the buses overcrowded with nuns and soldiers, so Maruja decides to splurge and take a taxi. The car is one of those pocket-sized asthmatic Seats, and the driver has to strap one suitcase to the roof and the other over the boot. We climb up a steep gradient, towards the city walls.

'That is the corral where the bulls are kept overnight before the run.' She points excitedly to the left.

We enter through imposing medieval gates and make our way into a maze of increasingly narrow streets.

'This is the first gangway the bulls use during San Fermín, remember last year?'

We stop in the heart of the old city, in a street so narrow that neighbours talk to each other from window to window, and share the same clothesline. Like everything about Maruja, her billfold is round and bulging at the seams. She pays with discoloured sweaty *pesetas* and offers the driver a healthy tip if he will carry our suitcases up for us.

'*Fíjate, soy la* Barefoot Contessa!'

The poster for that first-run movie shows a tall, glamorous woman in a risqué evening gown carrying her high heels. Neither of us has seen *The Barefoot Contessa*, but the poster epitomizes Maruja's hate–hate relationship with shoes, and whenever she carries them in her hand, she thinks of it.

'Ava Gardner copied me! I was doing this long before her.'

'The Barefoot Contessa is Sophia Loren.'

'No, Ava is more glamorous because she married Dominguín, the bullfighter.'

Maruja laughing, gingerly barefoot on cold tiles, is proof that we have come to the end of our journey.

The spiral staircase, even with the overhead light switched on, is dark and cold. The walls have that special incense smell one finds in cavernous churches. Each stone step is worn smooth in the middle from centuries of plodding feet. With nothing to carry, I fly up the three flights. Maruja lags behind.

Señora María Gonzalez is hard of hearing, but somehow she knows our taxi has arrived and she stands with her door ajar awaiting us. Perhaps perched at her tiny balcony she was watching for us. She greets us hunched over, with an expectant little smile on her thin lips. Small and square-shouldered and extremely dignified, she doesn't turn her neck. Her hair is just like Manolo's, thick and black, with a few strands of grey at the roots. I have never seen her comb it, never seen it any way other than in a perfect bun.

'*Qué muñeca linda, qué amor, mi muñeca de porcelana!*'

'—' Señora Gonzalez has a stoic, strong way of being silent that could easily pass for speech.

Maruja hugs her mother-in-law and keeps kissing her as if she were a long-lost china doll, and she keeps wiping her tears on the old woman's cheeks, a sort of homecoming present. Señora Gonzalez accepts Maruja's tears with a bemused smile on her face. In her quiet way, it is obvious the old lady appreciates all this mothering.

'Isn't she a beautiful doll, a pearl, a dream? Come on, guess, *niño*, guess how old this love-heart is? Look how white her skin is – not one wrinkle. Not a wrinkle!'

The kitchen, with a central square table wiped clean, has a funereal sunless quality. The floor is made up of large black and white tiles. There is no refrigerator, only a larder and a cold storage box. On a sideboard washed vegetables wait to be diced. Maruja's kitchen has never looked as immaculate or lifeless as this.

I wonder what goes on in this silent dark apartment during the eleven and a half months when we are not here – just the ticking of the grandfather clock?

'How was the trip?' asks Señora Gonzalez, her voice deep and sonorous like a man's.

Maruja asks a million questions, answers them, presents her mother-in-law with coffee and chocolate and tea (unfortunately the bulk we will take to Galicia). Maruja keeps interrupting herself, 'Señora Gonzalez, how did you become so beautiful? I swear if I hadn't just had *churros* and chocolate, I would eat you right up!'

Señora Gonzalez laughs without making a sound; only her shoulders rise and fall. 'What does the boy want to eat?' she asks.

'Nothing, thank you.'

'Do you want to eat, *niño*?' She fetches the cakes and cookies she has set aside for our arrival.

'Sit down, *señora*. Please sit.' Maruja keeps insisting. 'You are not my mother-in-law, you are queen for a day, OK?'

The overhead lights are dim, but in this apartment, where Manolo was born and grew up, I can make out the photo of his father. He looks like some parchment engraving, a wax figure who never smiled in his whole life, never made it out of the black framed portrait around which hangs a rosary. This home is a place full of shadows and silence, almost as restricted and polite as Manolo himself.

In a yellowed wedding photo I see Maruja beaming round-faced under a tall beehive hairdo, and Manolo looking lean and boyish.

I hear a polite cough in the living-room, one of those official rooms towards the front of the apartment one never enters. I become aware of a stranger standing in the shadows, staring at me. He does not move or say anything, but we stare at each other, waiting. It is weird beyond belief.

He turns out to be Manolo's older brother, a retired photographer, whom Manolo has refused to speak to for years. It is impossible to know exactly what caused this bad blood between the two brothers. 'A divorced don, a fornicator, *un marrano cochino jilipolla!*' is all I get out of Manolo. '*Un sinvergüenza!*' Maruja thinks it has to do with the fact that the brother steals money from their mother.

When I give him my hand to shake, I expect him to return it to me with a few fingers missing, but I am surprised to find him a rather charming roly-poly gentleman. He too, like Manolo, is bow-legged and shy, and his pants have a tendency to rumple at the ankles, but, try as I do, it is impossible to hate him. Maybe he was not spying on us from the living-room shadows, maybe he was scared Manolo might be with us, and was waiting for the right moment to introduce himself? I never meet him again.

Araceli, Manolo's lone sister, returns from the bakery where she works as a salesgirl. She brings us yet more fresh cakes, apple turnovers, chocolate éclairs. Seeing mother and daughter together, both wearing black, both smiling shyly and covering their mouths when they laugh, gives me a glimpse of the quiet years they have spent huddled here, their timid rituals, their orderly severe lives.

Maruja stacks cream cakes on to my plate, catching in her mouth a slip of chocolate. On vacation she treats me as one of her suitcases into which it is her duty to shove as much as she can. 'I've promised his mother that I am going to fatten him up at least ten kilos. The boy is nothing but bones.'

Araceli and her mother watch Maruja with dismay. Maruja, stage centre, is talking a mile a minute, she has taken over the spotless kitchen and is examining pots and pans, rearranging where various utensils should be kept. Everyone becomes a child when faced with Maruja's overwhelming mothering, even her aged mother-in-law.

'*El niño* has to eat!' repeats Maruja, 'and so do you two!' Soon she has all three of us seated and eating a soup of *caldo gallego*, leftovers.

After our mid-morning lunch, we head towards Pamplona's main cathedral. Today is a special feast on which the bishop of the city leads relics of San Fermín around the streets and personally gives communion to the faithful. The fact that the bishop himself is officiating somehow makes it more valuable, and the women do not want to miss it.

Araceli accompanies us through the crowded streets. She is taller than Maruja and lives here year-round, so I would expect her to lead the way, but it is Maruja on her round potato legs who spearheads us. To facilitate her walking, Maruja rips off the other heel; her high heels are now glorified slippers.

A city full of women is streaming towards the cathedral. Jostling each other. Running with one foot on the narrow sidewalk, the other in the street. Stopping traffic. We pass a group of Catholics standing in white hoods like the KKK, singing in Latin, and one of them is swinging a smoking incense-holder on a long silver chain. This madness reminds me of the Easter I spent here, when down the tiny streets came towering *papier-mâché* figures, witches and devils, but also Isabel and Ferdinand, Christopher Columbus and El Cid, Moorish horsemen and princesses, all of them giving out candies and cookies. Maruja held me tight and screamed into my ear. Only through fancy footwork did I escape being bashed by the witches' brooms.

Today, in the cathedral, the women in their black shawls and white *mantillas* press for a closer look at the reliquary. We arrive late for Mass and go directly to the altar, a huge overly ornate rococo gilt and bronze affair, thick with incense, dripping with cherubs and saints. We wait for almost half an hour as the bishop administers to all those kneeling at the wrought-iron railing. By the time we make it to the front, I have watched His Bishopness's lily-white hands give the host to three hundred and fifty mouths. I kneel. He approaches, surrounded by perfectly combed choirboys, dressed in long red robes with icy-white shoulder bibs. I can feel Maruja grow tense with admiration, she could eat these choirboys up in one gulp – they are exactly how she wants me to look. The white hands approach. I expect His White Handedness to run out of hosts just before he reaches me, because the line of faithful is endless, but he keeps dipping inside his golden chalice and coming up with an endless supply. I stick out my tongue. He deposits the wafer and moves on to Maruja and then to Araceli.

The sermon is about Saint Paul telling the Corinthians not to fornicate or engage in so much sensuality. We return to the street feeling holier and more blessed.

Back at the house, Señora Gonzalez begs us to stay but Maruja is eager to see her home. We leave one suitcase behind, and collect the keys to the apartment she and Manolo own on the outskirts of town.

Most of the taxis are down by the train station, so we take a bus instead. Each of us holds one rope of the suitcase, and between us it should feel lighter, but it has gained weight since we arrived. I suspect Manolo's mother of adding a part of her larder to the bulging side pockets. Maruja gets a kindly soldier to lift the bag up on to the bus.

We rumble out through the northern gate of the city. The sign says no talking to the driver, but Maruja stands at the front telling him about herself, and the weather, and how they drive in Paris, and within a few minutes she has him agreeing to drop us off closer to her apartment. Through the floorboards, in a hole under the gas pedal, I can see the tarmac racing by, and this sight makes the bus feel even flimsier than it looks – only the mounds of salty sunflower shells on the floorboards give it any sense of solidity at all. Around corners I keep expecting us to simply topple over. Buses going in the opposite direction seem to defy gravity by staying upright. Ours strains at maximum pitch, its lawnmower whine shifting into higher dyspeptic decibels. Soldiers and schoolgirls try staying upright as the centrifugal force leans them and shakes them together. Manolo claims he learned what he knows about women from riding on crowded city buses. We pass a large sugar factory and the air is filled with a fetid smell.

We are home, or almost home.

Maruja and Manolo's house is a fifth-floor walk-up in a seven-floor cement high-rise block of flats that makes up one of Pamplona's new northernmost districts.

Climbing the five floors dragging our anvil-suitcase is hard going. Maruja stops on each landing and waits for her heart to calm down. When she arrives in front of her door, she is so excited to be home she kneels and kisses the unpainted cement doorstep. From here we can see the foothills of the Pyrenees, and curling out from behind one large hill the train tracks leading towards the main city depot. This area of arid stony ground, with a few shrubs and disused train sidings and a junk-heap, is my play yard. It is here in summer along a winding disused road that I chase basking lizards, trying to stamp on their tails.

Maruja and Manolo have decorated and equipped this apartment with their lifelong earnings. They have drowned it with all the love and care they would give a child if they had one.

The chairs and couches still bear the clear plastic slip-covers from the store where they were bought. The toilet seat is a spongy white foam that you sink into and which slowly reflates when you get off, a singularly unpleasant sensation. I keep imagining the compression of other buttocks on this tired foam.

Maruja's pride is the shiny lacquered rosewood armoire in her living-room which displays all her cheap wedding gifts and fancy china. The commode smells of wood varnish and you can't open the doors without the varnished pale wood creaking and threatening to fall apart. Her first instinct is to make certain that none of her porcelain has been stolen and then to dust it. No one ever eats on that 'nice' china. We use the chipped kitchen plates.

Above my sagging bed, the silver crucifix has a sprig of dead palms left over from last year's Palm Sunday. The bed is narrow and pushed up against the sideboard.

Maruja heaps blankets on top of me. The weight of each one falling, woof woof, adding to the layers already crushing me, gives me confidence, buries me in warmth. The house smells different, strange. I would feel homesick without Maruja, but she knows all my pleasures, all my fears. (My only real loathing is the remedial summer maths I am meant to do.) Travel-ripe farts burn a hole in my sheets. I don't dare smell them accumulating, trapped under so many layers. But a little odour never bothered Maruja.

She kisses me goodnight, 'If you have a nightmare you are welcome in my big double bed, *niño*.'

I fall asleep immediately.

33

CHAPTER FOUR

The flip-flop wars

Maruja on vacation is the same as Maruja at work. She goes shopping, she fills the fridge, she prepares huge meals. She never stops. Manolo joins us, and Maruja keeps him busy buying things for the house and fixing the place up. It is endless work, but they devote all their love and energy to this immaculate two-bedroom apartment full of sunshine.

She spends much of the day in her modern kitchen, gloating about how much bigger, cleaner and airier it is than ours in Paris. 'All the plumbing works,' she says, flushing just for the joy of hearing it go down, an obvious counterpoint to Parisian plumbing. 'And look at the sky, not a single cloud! That is the kind of sky I like, a Spanish sky!'

Maruja often sits there smiling, just enjoying the airiness and the sunlight. Her square window looks out on to rows of clotheslines where towels and sheets flap between two high-rises. She leans there, eyes closed, letting the sun warm her and the wind blow in her hair.

The kitchen is shiny with white tiles, except for one horizontal row of tiny rectangular tiles which are painted in vegetable motifs: salad, cucumber, spinach, beet, Brussels sprouts, corn, cabbage, aubergine – Maruja is especially pleased with this touch, and every year she seeks new vegetables to add to her tile collection. The walls and sink are spanking clean, used only a few weeks every summer. A large blue canister of butane gas under the sink is empty, and while ordering a replacement, Maruja heats the stove with firewood.

She organizes picnics by a stream, and Manolo, slipping and sliding on the rocks, teaches me to catch fresh-water shrimps that Maruja immediately shells and adds to our steaming *paella*.

I spend many an afternoon in the fields behind the building. Here, past the play yard and the broken swing set, behind the last high-rise, after the junk-yard and the train tracks, the northern suburb ends and the open countryside begins. The no-man's-land where a city stops and nothing begins is oddly moving and dramatic. Everything in this scrub land suddenly becomes personal and private. Here there are big wide lazy wheatfields, and no one in the city seems to care what goes on here. I play along a disused farm road that slopes gently upwards.

Chasing lizards is a sport Manolo shows me. It is not an enormous amount of fun, it is sort of stupid in fact, but once you start dashing around, slamming your foot down on everything that moves, every tail, every shadow – there are hundreds of lizards to aim at – it becomes addictive and you find yourself playing it for hours. The enormously bored reptiles cover every flat stone of the disused road, and they race off into cracks and crevices, as fast in retreat as they are to reappear after I step away. It's their disregard for me that enchants me. I never succeed in stamping on any of them, but once I do notice a little green tail that has so little life it could be a twig. It lies there all by itself on the rocks. Shocked, I search in vain for its tailless owner, whom I expect to see limping about like a car with a flat tyre, but he is nowhere.

'*Mataste la lagartija! Mataste la, cobarde!*' laughs Manolo.

'*No fui yo.*'

'*Sí, sí, tú, tú!*'

I don't believe Manolo's explanation that losing a tail does not hurt them in the slightest and that it grows back like a fingernail. After all, it is Manolo who has explained to me that babies come from women spilling a black liquid into men and getting the men in trouble. (Maruja's gales of laughter when I recount this indicate that whatever the real mechanism is, Manolo is not to be trusted.)

Maruja makes me wear flip-flops because she wants my feet to breathe, to get healthy and full of sunlight after the lead exhaust of the city, but those flip-flops render my lizard-hunting all the more improbable for they forever fly off, and my heels end up stomping naked on the rock.

Rubber flip-flops are considered girly shoes in Spain, and on my way out through the play yard, as my fwap

36

fwap echoes against the high-rise walls, I catch much abuse from the boys hanging out there. Obnoxious wolf whistles and doubts about my manhood. Flip-flopping in silence is difficult – only a single thong between the big toe and index toe holds them on. But a flat-footed shuffle ensures that the sole does not slap up against the bottom of my heel and allows me to lift the sandal up and push it forward silently until I place it down on the next step. This method of travel requires dexterity and works only for short distances, usually while I am passing in front of bullies. But when I am alone, I resort to my shameless fwap-fwap sissy walk.

José, a neighbour's son, who is my age, asks, 'Why don't you get Maruja to buy you a new pair of leather sandals, like mine?'

'I am American,' I explain.

'Yeah, so what?'

'Well, I don't mind what other people say.'

The real reason I don't complain to Maruja is that back in my school sandals are definitely uncool, and I know that as long as mine are rubber and cheap there is no risk of them returning with us to Paris and anyone arguing that I should wear them to school. Whereas if we go to Bata and buy a fancy pair of leather sandals, they will follow me wherever I go, and my brothers will see them, and my friends in school, and my neighbours, and the whole civilized world will know for sure I am an asshole and the ignominy will be impossible to live down.

José's older brother has become a Franciscan monk, and we visit him in his monastery. The monks are playing soccer, and it is rather ridiculous all these strong men in their brown skirts, heading the ball, dribbling, shooting. I notice they too wear leather sandals; everyone in Spain does. José's mother and father give him sandwiches and bottles of olive oil for the monastery. But when we leave, his mother cries. She keeps telling José to avoid this fate.

He is a soft-spoken shy boy who borders on being too polite, too well brought up by his parents. (Ten years later José will also become a monk.) He knows the area, but it is I who lead him around and teach him a life of crime. I take him to the train tracks where we are not allowed to go, and we place one-*peseta* coins and one-*duro* and five-*duro* pieces face up on the shiny silver tracks, and then we hide down the embankment. After the train passes and the acrid smoke dies down, we collect the flattened money. Franco has disappeared. In place of his military uniform and round face there is a shiny blankness, smooth as a mirror. José worries that this is sacrilegious and illegal. We are destroying money – if it catches on, the country will be in chaos.

I teach José to climb into the apple trees and steal apples. We eat them there, greedily, while spying on women collecting their wash. According to José, the manager of the junk-yard is an old drunken bastard who will kill us if we go near his rotten domain. I dare José. At first he refuses. But there is little else to do in no-man's-land. Soon we are climbing up piles of bald tyres, pulling up old door handles, broken toilets, great hills of broken junk, stuff that has no front, no back, no sideways, when suddenly the bastard appears, a tiny dot in the distance, standing by his single-room pine hut from which smoke curls day and night. The old bastard shouts. His two huge German shepherds, barking, take off towards us. José, who knows these dogs, races across the junk-yard, back under the electric wire fence, and heads towards the orchard.

I do not move. I doubt I can make it to the trees wearing my flip-flops – I certainly cannot run over the piles of junk without losing one or both of my sandals and cutting my bare feet on steel and glass. Another reason I do not run is that I am terrified. I watch those two dogs bounding towards me, hounds from hell, the Baskerville pair, their teeth scissoring the air, and I am paralysed with fear. This has never happened to me before. The dogs are getting bigger by the second. I am at the south end of the junk-yard, not far from the electric fence. But the killers are so single-mindedly headed for me, so forcefully targeted on me, I feel like a roadkill hypnotized by headlights.

Even now I could turn and dash under the fence, get as far as the public path that borders the junk-yard so that when the dogs maul me they will be in the wrong, but I feel ridiculous turning after so many seconds of waiting.

The waiting is endless. What am I doing standing here, waiting for these man-eaters? I see José leap on to the first branch of the apple tree, and keep climbing as high as he dares as if not even gravity can stop the dogs.

I don't want to admit my fear, don't want to give the dogs more incentive to chase me. I almost feel brave waiting here without moving, as if I have some sort of right to be here, on the bastard's property. I want him to know I was doing nothing wrong. The dogs are so powerful, they are quite beautiful to watch. I hear the bastard's voice, calling them back. He is calling them by name, but they don't pay any heed, they keep coming. The two are only a hundred yards away, eighty, seventy, sixty, and the man is calling them. What if they don't stop? José is screaming at me from the trees:

'Don't be an imbecile, run, run! *Rápido, vete rápido!*'

The dogs shudder to a halt five feet away, but their speed is such that stopping brings them about two feet away. I can feel their hot breath on my face, their warm spittle. They are barking and slobbering so loud I want to shit in my pants. I am dead. These dogs are taller than I am. It would take them a single bite to kill me. I try to stand with as much dignity as I can to show I am not scared, but the fact that they have stopped is so miraculous, if I could I would kiss the bastard's feet. His control over these killers is miraculous. I slowly retreat. This is my first encounter with brute force. There is no possible arguing, no ability to finesse or salvage honour with such non-stop barking. I am lucky to be alive. As I move away towards the orchard, I feel sick and stupid. My instincts were all wrong. Why did I stand there? Why did I think I could somehow tough it out? José up in his tree is white.

'You are crazy!'

'Yes.'

'They were going to eat you!'

'Yes!'

'Why didn't you run? I told you to run.'

'I don't know.'

After the episode with the dogs, I don't see José any more. A few days later, I am again behind the high-rises, beyond the junk-yard, away from the train tracks, busy stomping at lizard chimeras. My attempts are half-hearted. A couple of toughs appear. They are about my age, but taller, the gypsy boys who whistled at my flip-flops earlier. They seem happy to see me, as if they had been searching for me.

'*Hola*,' says one.

'*Hola*,' I respond, shading my eyes.

'*Hola, chica*, what pretty ladylike slippers you have!'

'*Chica*,' says the other. '*Chica, chica, chica*.'

I don't tell them, *Come mierda, jilipolla*. I wait, squinting into the sunlight.

One of them picks a long stick from an old paint can of tar I hadn't noticed before, and he tries painting tar on my back. I hit the stick away, but the other one uses another stick to slap me and tar my head. I go at them with both fists, but their sticks keep me at bay. The toughs laugh. I shield myself with my hands, but their sticks make my arms sticky and black with tar. As soon as I get one to run away, the other attacks from behind. I feel like a bull in a bullring. They keep picking up new sticks. After a while, the two tire and leave me.

I am not too hurt. It could have been worse. As I walk home, I feel quite proud of myself, chasing away two toughs by myself. In my mind I go over the scenario, how I fought them off, how I managed to lunge and grab one stick out of one of the boy's hands. And the other. I am full of pride and ready to aggrandize my role to suit my tale.

Maruja's screams fill the apartment. 'My God, what did they do to you, *pobrecito, pobrecito, pobre amor mio!!!*'

They were brutes, she repeats, they were animals. How many of them were there? She removes my clothes and puts me in a bath. I have tar all up and down my body. She cuts my hair short. I tell her how well I fought, but she robs me, she spreads the word to all her neighbours that a bunch of gypsy lowlifes put me through the wringer. What was a stunning victory becomes a signal defeat. For weeks people stop me and ask about the whipping I received.

The only positive result of this fight is that the flip-flops get thrown out along with everything else full of tar.

There is a hidden side to Manolo. Adults think of him as a deaf mute, but around me he is a non-stop talker and prankster. One morning when I am lying in Maruja's bed keeping warm, he dips his hand down under the covers and, howling with laughter, pulls out a handful of Maruja's pubic hairs. 'Here, look! It is harvest time in my wife's forest.'

Maruja keeps pushing her nightgown down, shouting, 'Stop, stop. *Asqueroso, cochino, cerdo, marrano!*' She laughs.

'I am going to make a pillow from her pubic hair.'

'Keep your hands to yourself, you bandit.'

I don't ask where these hairs come from, and I don't want to know. Manolo is the most timid man I know with others. I don't think I have ever heard him speak more than two words to my father. When there are guests at the house, my favourite trick is to call Manolo into the living-room and get a big blowzy American to ask him a question, just to see his face go red.

In the Bois de Boulogne my new battery-operated boat gets stuck in a stagnant green waterway. And the stones I throw to get it back only push the red outboard motor further away. I don't care for the boat, but to cause Manolo trouble I scream that my uncle just gave it to me, that it is my favourite boat, and I demand that he go fetch it. Red with shame, he removes his pants and shirt and, with people passing on all sides, he wades out into that black and putrid water. I laugh with glee and call attention to him. Manolo hides half-naked behind some bushes because he is embarrassed by the passers-by. After that he devises ever more sophisticated ways of avoiding my traps. Only when we are completely alone does Manolo open up.

Today he takes a break from house-fixing and leads me on a long walk. It is a sizzling day. We pass the junk-yard, pass the spot where I was tarred. We follow the lizard road north into the foothills until it becomes just a narrow path. We climb all day. It is exhausting. The path winds through arid scrub and stony brushland. Eventually we climb into a pine forest. Butterflies, their yellow and orange wings mirroring the heat, are everywhere. The air is loaded with the scent of heather and jasmine, wild mint, lemon grass, fennel. It's so hot at midday, even the birds go quiet.

We reach another ridge, turn around and see the group of high-rises where we live spread out at our feet, and beyond it a haze of industrial pollution from the tall stacks of the sugar factory, and then the walled town of Pamplona.

He tells me endless stories. The same stories he fills my head with when he accompanies me on the bus to school. It's odd that a man who never talks can be so full of words. Usually he tells of wars, wars for walled cities, with heroes who whip chariots over gaping chasms and leap boulders and slay dragons.

Today he tells me a wild tale of King Canute fighting the barbarians. The castle is defended by 10,000 Huns with pots of steaming burning oil, and Canute is all alone. He has to get into the city, to save the five beautiful virgins who have been made prisoner and are languishing chained to the walls of their cells, and he has to do this before the Huns rape and eat the women.

'How do you think Canute does it?'

'With planes and tanks?' I say, wondering where such a shy, quiet man with perfectly styled hair gets such stories. He never reads books, never opens a newspaper.

'No, he has no modern weapons, just his bare hands.'

'Is Canute alone?'

'Yes, all alone. But he is very strong.'

'I don't know. How? Tell me.'

Manolo smiles. 'First Canute takes a chariot with five strong horses, and he charges through the city gate with a battering ram. Then he escapes with thousands of Huns in hot pursuit, and as they follow him, he leads them over hidden elephant traps where he has buried sharp spikes and left a nest of lethal black adders. Five thousand die. Then he bends back twelve palm trees and sends a wave of coconuts crashing over the battlements into the central guardhouse. Another thousand die. Then he races right into the midst of the remaining barbarians, riding between the horses so that none of them can shoot at him or hurt him, and he throws steel balls so hard they cut the chains off the waiting virgins. Freed from their cell, these blondes jump on his chariot and help him torch the walled city, and he makes it out to safety just in the nick of time before all the powder kegs explode.'

I hound him for details. How big are the elephant traps, how many Huns can fit on the end of a pungi spike, how long does it take to die from the bite of a black adder? In public I can usually embarrass him and get him to blush, but in private, just the two of us, he has it all over me. And he knows it.

Our climb up the forest path leads us to a summit on the last ridge and from there it is downhill into a green valley. We have finished our *chorizo* sandwiches and our orange-ades, and, parched with thirst, we half run down the mountain.

'There's a beautiful clear river here.'

'You're lying.'

'No, have faith. Have I ever led you wrong?'

'All the time.'

When we reach the valley floor it is late afternoon, and the summer heat is finally starting to drop.

The narrow river is bordered on both sides by tall poplars. It is surely one of the most Edenesque sights I have ever seen. Manolo leads me to where it widens into a pool about three by five metres wide. There we bathe.

His feet are hairy and for some reason his index toe overlaps on the other as if he was tortured as a child. We swim in our underpants. The mountain water is so clear and fresh we lie there like two old dogs watching the trace of silver minnows slicing past us. My boxer shorts billow white in the current, Manolo wears tiny bikini briefs that make his white body look ridiculous. There is nothing to bother our warm midsummer idyll. Above us, poplar leaves fret and susurrate with the heat.

A little downriver a couple is swimming. This gives Manolo an excuse to discuss what men and women do when they think no one is watching. The couple suddenly become very still. We watch them embrace. Then they become even more still.

'Look at them.'

'What are they doing?'

'Making babies.'

'How do you know?'

'Because there are only two types of women, those who make babies and those who are dead.'

We watch the couple get dressed and leave. It grows late.

We wait for a bus connection at a crossroads, and now we ride with a pack of day labourers returning home. As soon as we are around other people, Manolo becomes a tomb. He keeps checking his watch. I try bucking him up: 'Don't worry, I'll tell Maruja it was my fault. That I took you to the river.'

He smiles, but it is half-hearted. We both know he will have to pay for this. I am thinking of all the times I have taken advantage of Manolo, and how everyone takes advantage of him. We ride, side by side, in the crowded bus. He smiles quietly at me. He is far too good for this world and for his own good.

'It was really great today, Manolo!'

'We'll do it again,' he says, certain that Maruja is going to keep him on a short leash from now on.

'We could try some other paths.'

'I know these hills like the back of my hand, you'll see, I'll take you up and down. Today was nothing.'

'It was great.'

'Oh, there are some secluded spots that make that little valley today look like the Place de la Concorde at rush-hour.'

It is dinner time, and in every village we pass, heavy olive oil cooking odours waft over us. Frying *chorizo*, garlic, onions, potatoes, *paellas*. Maruja's dinner will be getting cold, waiting for us. We both can taste it. Any time I smell olive oil I think of Maruja and get hungry.

'She'll be steaming mad.'

'Yeah.'

CHAPTER FIVE

Manolo days

Hanging out with him in a city is much less fun than tramping through the countryside together.

He is so shy, he walks down the sidewalk as if embarrassed to take up too much room and breathe in someone else's air. His eyes have that evasive look as if he is ready, at any moment, to give anyone the spot on which he is standing. He's lived in Pamplona all his life, but he has no favourite corner, no special hangout. We walk the streets like two refugees.

It is only because Maruja is sick and tired of having us in the house, and does not want me to play cards any more, that she has shooed us out into the street. 'Go into town,' she said. 'I don't want to see you all day.'

Well, now we are in town, and neither of us have any idea what we should do next.

When I am in Paris with Manolo, he is usually accompanying me to and from school, and so he can concentrate on telling me stories and goofing off, but today we are paralysed with having to select a destination and a fate.

'What do you want to do?' he keeps asking.

'I don't know, what do you want to do?'

'I don't know. Anything.'

'Yeah. Like what?'

'I am happy we are not at home.'

'Yeah, the last spring cleaning she did I thought she was going to throw out the walls. She was hysterical.'

It is Sunday morning, and we are lucky Maruja has not asked us to help in one of her famous top-to-bottom house cleanings, but having nothing to do isn't easy. Especially for Manolo, who is used to following orders.

He keeps walking straight ahead, but if I stop, or point him in another direction, he follows me – this is what most terrifies me. He has no idea where we are going. He even lets me take charge! Only Manolo's overwhelming timidity gives us any sort of guidance at all.

We enter a large open-air market and make our way into a central wrought-iron edifice in the middle of the square. The women here calling out prices and holding up a piece of meat for sale make Maruja look and sound like a crown princess. We have no business here, but the press of bodies and the hub of activity fills our silence and gives us something to do. We climb up to the first floor and find all sorts of animals for sale: ducks, chickens, rabbits, pigeons, canaries, goats, piglets, lambs, peacocks, goldfish.

'I want a canary, Manolo, I promise I'll take care of it.'

'No pets are allowed in our high-rise.'

'Well, we'll sneak him in.'

'Oh no, we'd get evicted.'

'How about a goldfish, they're easy to take care of. They shit in the water.'

'Will you change the water?'

'Sure, if we take him back to Paris. How about a gerbil?'

We watch customers haggle over price. Buyers are checking the teeth of a lamb and its eyes. The rabbits look scared. The chickens are tied by their feet and held upside down. I wonder how long they can stand that sort of treatment.

'Isn't it cruel, Manolo?'

'Well, at least it's fresher meat than what they have downstairs. They're still alive.'

'Want to bring one back to Maruja?'

'Maybe.'

'Hey, we could buy her dinner, she would really like that. And buying them live is like a third cheaper, right?'

'Maybe half price.'

Manolo and I have so little to do that pricing these creatures creates a bond between us, a tightness.

Manolo only has five hundred *pesetas* to spare on him, which is about four dollars — not much, but enough. He puts the money back into his pocket carefully. Without Maruja around to yell at him, all his gestures are tenuous, as if he does not want to make a mistake.

Bumming around town with Manolo is a study in tentativeness and defensiveness: everything in the street —

lights changing, a motor scooter passing, a woman carrying shopping bags – takes precedence over him. I wonder how Manolo does it, displaces so little air, formulates so few opinions about anything. I never understand what it is that so terrifies him in other people. This makes us inseparable – Manolo and me.

I ask him for a chocolate ice-cream. It is the boys' day out, and it feels special to be without Maruja, just on our own. I ask him to tell me a story.

He takes me up to the city machicolations and there, sitting at the battlements overlooking the valley and the foothills, he teaches me a lot of things. He teaches me, for instance, that Santa Claus likes to wear women's clothes and is wanted for questioning by the morals police. He explains what cross-dressing is. (To me it all sounds invented and improbable, but with Manolo I never know what to believe.) He explains that some men like to make love to animals, that he was once engaged to be married to a snake. That a snake would have been an improvement on Maruja. That in the army he once made love with a camel and once with a giraffe; they put him on a ladder so he could get his penis into the poor beast.

'You are such a liar! Get off it!'

'I am telling you the God's honest truth. And in Galicia, in Maruja's village, the men there regularly make love to calves.'

'Come on, for once in your life tell me the truth!'

'I am! Calves suck on a finger, a teat, anything. You

remember that calf that had lost its mother, we fed it with a milk bottle?'

'Yes.'

'Well, it's the same thing.'

I am wondering how other children get their sexual education. Why does mine have to be so haphazard, so skewed?

'No, seriously,' says Manolo, 'one day I bit Maruja's nipples off, and they had to be sewn back on.'

I walk away in disgust. But for all his lying, he is a fount of important information. Thanks to him I know what the visual panty-line under a woman's dress says about her muscles, the firmness of her buttocks. And why elevators smell different to midgets. Why farting is healthy. And why rich people are less kind than poor people.

We head back to the central market square. In the crowded streets, Manolo does not look like Canute, he doesn't look like much of anything, the way he fumbles to make certain he still has the money in his pocket.

We find two large white chickens going for five hundred and fifty *pesetas*. They seem like a good buy. They are white and look big, bigger than all the others. Manolo talks the man down to five hundred.

'They must be juicy.'

'Yeah, they look fat and healthy.'

'Try to get him down some more.'

'I tried already.'

Manolo hands over his single large-denomination bill, and we head for home. The chickens are heavy, and we take turns carrying them. They were a great idea in the market place, surrounded by other animals tied up, but the further we go on the bus home, the more ridiculous I feel dragging two birds around.

Neither Manolo nor I have ever bought a live animal to eat. In the past it was always pets – parakeets, mice, gerbils, guinea-pigs, rabbits, ducks, lizards – and I always rushed to give them names and figure out if they were males or females. But this is different. I carry these chickens upside down from a rope, and I try acting like they are already dead. A few times one gets excited and tries spreading his clipped wings, but otherwise they don't seem to mind being upside down.

Both of us are proud of having the guts and foresight of choosing such a gift for Maruja, and we ring the doorbell with an enormous sense of anticipation.

'*Qué, dos gallinas viejas?*' Maruja laughs and watches Manolo deposit them on the kitchen sink. 'They're older than Methuselah! I'll have to boil them three hours.' She can't stop laughing. 'Why didn't you get smaller, tenderer chickens? These are stone-hard. They were already old before the flood.'

Then in the kitchen she screams. 'They have lice! Oh my God, get them out of the house, put them on the balcony. Didn't you check them? They're alive with vermin. And who is going to kill them?'

Manolo and I stare at each other in horror.

'And who'll pluck them?'

I am starting to feel ill at the thought of white feathers and ticks floating round the room.

Maruja, wiping sweat from her face, says: 'I don't mind wringing their necks, I did that all my youth, it is plucking them that I hate. Manolo, you do it.'

That afternoon I stay out later than usual hopping around on the lizard stones. I return at dinner time. The roosters are in the large steel-rimmed pressure cooker. She has made a stew out of them and she claims they will be as hard as old shoes.

But they're not that bad. Not half as bad as Maruja makes them out to be. I try not to think of Manolo sitting on a balcony full of swirling white feathers.

Later that night I ask Manolo why he can't have babies.

'Because she won't let me put it all the way in.'

'No, come on, tell me the truth.'

'That's the God's honest truth.'

'Put what in where?'

'To have babies, a man has to insert his balls into a woman.'

'Naaaaaaah, come on, tell me the truth.' I'm laughing, but the thing about Manolo's lies is they might just be true.

'And all Maruja allows me is just the very tip.'

'Huh? The tip of what?'

'A centimetre or two of me, and that's not enough.'

'So what will you do?'

'I don't know.'

'Will you adopt?'

'That's what Maruja wants.'

'Maybe she is too fat to have babies?'

'Maybe I pulled out too many of her bush hairs?'

'Why, what does that do?'

'I'm not sure, but things are extremely complex down there.'

'No, really, what do the doctors say?'

'They say I have to keep at her until the stork comes.'

'No, come on, be serious just for once in your life.'

'That is what they say, but she always has a headache, or she is not feeling well, or she's having a nervous breakdown.'

Reading Manolo is like trying to understand Latin spoken in sign language. I don't think he has ever spoken a straight word to me in his life. I keep pulling on his arms to get him to stop and pay serious attention to me. 'Don't lie, come on.'

'I'm serious, I swear it on the head of my noble mother, may she drop dead this minute if I am not telling you God's honest truth. So help me God, cross my heart and hope to die.' He is as serious as a priest, then smiles to indicate he is lying.

'She's so fat, how will we know if she gets pregnant?'

'Well, if you hear Maruja screaming in bed, *AAAAAII-*

IIEeeeeee, más más más más más, then you will know I have succeeded.'

'Don't be disgusting.'

Manolo never enters Araceli's bakery with me. It's not clear why, but a dozen times we find ourselves passing right in front of it, and I stop. But Manolo keeps his head turned and keeps on walking.

'Come on, let's go inside and say hello.'

'No, I am not hungry.'

'Don't be shy, Araceli won't eat you. She likes visits.'

'No, you go in if you want, I'll go home.'

Hoping he will follow me, I charge into the store, but he doesn't follow. I am alone with Araceli. And I am not ready for this. I imagine Manolo waiting outside, hiding, rushing away down the street as fast as he can.

It's different alone, without Maruja at my side to fill in the deep silences and to chatter on about nothing.

In the middle of a dusty, long-drawn-out shopping day, in the midst of rushing, with Maruja's heart giving her palpitations and her hands sweatier than usual, we often find ourselves right in front of Araceli's bakery. Inside we find an oasis of smiles and coolness out of the midday heat. A chance for Maruja to take her flat shoes off and rub her tired feet.

Jelly doughnuts without any holes are the most popular. And Araceli, in her wispy timid way behind the shiny glass counter, takes great pleasure in giving me anything I want. The ritual is always the same: I decline politely, knowing full well she will disgorge all the puddings, apple turnovers and chocolate pies I want.

The two other employees in that gloomy, empty bakery take as much joy in my eating as Araceli does. The cashier is covered in cobwebs, she gives change with all the dignity of a paraplegic working an abacus. The other sales lady, a deaf mute I believe, sits against the wall under a portrait of Franco. Once I actually see her get up and go to check the ovens in the back, but she returns and sits down empty-handed.

Araceli, in her mid fifties, is the youngest of the three and therefore she stands nearest the door; she is the one who leaps in sprightly manner to answer the demands of the clientele.

When Maruja and I enter this store we bring all the life and truth of the street into a place of mortuary silence. The saleswomen watch us and listen with the fascination of children attending a circus. The street is too narrow for the sun ever to reach inside the bakery, and the three women languish here like hydroponic plants deprived of sunlight.

'*Qué ricos estan los pastelitos, que Dios te bendiga!*' says Maruja, swallowing her third apple turnover.

Araceli is shy and blushes easily. Her hair, far thinner than Manolo's, is always done up in a bouffant, teased style. At the top of her forehead, tiny spit curls somehow free themselves from her chignon and give her a girlish, rebellious look that the rest of her appearance in her simple black dress belies. The tip of her nose is pink, the skin between her nostrils is so thin it's almost see-through.

With the approach of the July fiesta, the streets of Pamplona fill up with foreigners. Standing and eating Araceli's treasure trove, I hear screams and songs of fiesta revellers. Their drums and shouts shake the storefront window as they pass, distant maenads and bacchantes passing a sanctuary where antique temple virgins hide.

Once in a while tourists actually enter. They assume foolishly that this is a pastry shop like any other. They stand there sweaty and large, knowing nothing, not even Spanish, their feet swimming in dusty sandals. Their tie-dyed T-shirts and shorts and backpacks fill the store with flashy colours, and Araceli responds with a fervour of activity. She seldom actually speaks to them, she just bows to what the Americans and Swedes point to, then rushes to comply. Usually the foreigners want sandwiches, and this always drives Araceli into a tizzy because the bakery has no standard sandwich, and to prepare a custom-made sandwich requires time and patience. What Americans have trouble with is the concept that Araceli can put in it anything they want. This requires many questions. When I am there I translate, but I have spied on her through the window blushing and nodding in total ignorance, rushing to comply with demands she does not understand. As for payment, these big oxes open their palm and Araceli, with the precision of a small bird, picks out the coins needed.

Only when they leave does she relax and breathe normally again. She is happiest standing with her back to the wall watching me eat, listening to Maruja's gab and saying nothing at all. When Maruja starts opening her various shopping bags and packages, the bakery becomes alive, with all three ladies checking out Maruja's taste and confirming that she has made the right purchase.

We leave with our hands full of pastries. It is never clear whether Araceli has to pay for these out of her pocket at a reduced rate or whether they are on the house. But the latter seems more likely because no one keeps track of how much we eat.

It is a good address to have when you are broke, or tired, or don't know what else to do in the city. The problem is the small-talk you have to exchange with Araceli.

Now that Manolo has left me I am alone eating custard pies, and Araceli is standing there smiling, waiting for me to say something. 'So you have been out and about?'

'Yes, with Manolo, stomping on lizards again.'

'Oh, how interesting. Catch any?'

'No . . . actually, we don't really try.'

'No?'

'No . . . And we went swimming in a river the other day.'

'Oh, which river?'

'I don't know its name. It was more like a stream.'

'Was it nice?'

'Yeah, real nice.'

'What else are you doing in our city?'

'Oh, you know, the usual.'

'Here, have another éclair.'

'Thanks, no, I can't. They're very good, well, yes, OK, I'll have another. OK.'

All three ladies stare at me as I shove another madeleine into my mouth and chew, my mouth far too full to be able to speak.

CHAPTER SIX

San Fermín

Maruja dresses me up in the traditional outfit – the white cloth sandals with rope soles and long criss-crossing red laces that tie up and around the ankle (*alpargatas*), white pants, white shirt, a wide bright red sash that one wears wrapped around the waist as a belt (*faja*), and a half-litre leather wine gourd (*bota*). The wet comb she drags across my head leaves deep cleat marks in my hair. To Maruja, cleanliness is next to godliness, and she can't stop kissing me and hugging me. Dirt (the joys of mediocrity) she can't stand.

On the central square she pays a professional photographer to snap a shot of me, standing alone facing the sun. I stand there like one of those spotless San Fermín puppets you see hanging from the rear-view mirrors. She mails one photo to my parents and keeps the other in her wallet to show me off to her family and girlfriends. I am hers, the product of her love and attention. In a city of drunken debauchery, I am her Kewpie doll, her perfect soldier. Like the Spanish flag, like the bullring, and like San Fermín himself, patron saint of all the revellers, I am etched in bright red.

The first morning of the fiesta, 7 July, Manolo stays in bed and sleeps late. He has grown up with this, and to him the annual debauch is a nauseating spectacle. Like my father he considers bullfighting cruel and unnecessary.

Maruja wakes me up at sunrise, and we rush out of the house, for once without washing or eating breakfast. A gasping bus with cracks in the floorboards takes us to the city, not the north-west gate where the bull corral is located, because that road is cut off, but a nearby gate. The sun, just clearing the rooftops and bouncing off the orange roof-tiles, turns so bright it is refracted to us as shiny bronze.

We take a long, circuitous route and enter a house on Calle de la Estafeta that belongs to one of Araceli's friends. It is a dark apartment with two windows facing the narrow street. The old woman who lives there is seated at her kitchen table in her bathrobe, sipping coffee. She sits in the dark and waves us to the window. 'Go, go, we'll talk later.'

I am pressed up between the narrow wrought-iron flowers of the small balcony in front of me and Maruja's oversize bosoms pushing from behind.

Leaning out over me, Maruja chats with other ladies leaning at windows on either side of us. Down below us, about ten metres directly below the balcony, I can see men milling around, some walking down the hill. If I crane way out I can see the city gates down at the bottom of the hill, and the big wooden portals that mark the emplacement of the old drawbridge, and the wimples of nuns gathering to pray. Because there are no houses in front of us, the city battlements describe a big circle towards the north-east and spread out before us in long slanting shadows, the heart of the old city with its jumble of tightly-packed chimneys and its ubiquitous clotheslines, flapping in the wind.

The sky is pale blue, and the air is beginning to warm up.

The first *cohete* or firecracker shoots up from the roof of the city hall with a loud woosh. Maruja points to its dusty curlicue tail hanging in the sky above the churches for a moment before it explodes.

'*Aie aie aie aie,*' she screams, her excitement communicating itself to me through her breasts and her steel-ribbed bra pushing into my neck. '*Aie! Solamente queda un minuto!*'

The *cohete* and her *aie-aies* jolt the runners. Some stare up at us and wave. The foreigners, English, German, Scandinavian and American boys, take a last swig of wine from their leather wine gourds, check their shoelaces. (Some wear red T-shirts or windbreakers out of ignorance or stupidity.) The experienced Pamplonicos carry a newspaper rolled up lengthwise to tap the nose of the bull in order to try and distract him if one comes too close. They look like condemned prisoners, down there in the narrow cobblestone street without windows, without any exits.

'*Aie aie aie!*' I feel Maruja's heart beating faster.

It is not hot, but I can feel she has started to sweat. From my perspective, staring down, it is hard to tell which men are tall and which are short – they are all flat against the cobblestones. And they are massed in such a crowd it seems hard to believe they will be able to run. I wonder if this is how God sees us, antlike, scurrying around on the surface of the earth.

They were walking down towards the city portals but now they walk back up the hill, staring over their shoulders.

The second *cohete* goes up higher, it twists up, roman candle style, and the explosion high above the rooftops leaves an imperceptible flash that is swallowed by the morning rays. Maruja's hands clutch the balustrade. A woman at the balcony on our right throws out a rope ladder.

Down below, the entire street is moving up the hill. None of those starting here has a hope of reaching the bullring seven kilometres away in the centre of town, but this spot is for the bravest, those who've been here before.

Unlike the rest of the course, here the walls are sheer. There are no police barricades and no place to throw yourself, or hide if the bulls catch up. Women of mercy from their flowered balconies join Maruja in her syncopated *aie aie aies*! Their screams and rope ladders are the only escape route now.

The bulls are nowhere in sight, but one can hear their

65

rumbling on the cobblestones, or perhaps it is Maruja's heartbeat pounding into my back.

The men are running fast now. Turning the corner at the city gates, suddenly the first bull appears. They are charging up a street they have never seen before, but they speed along Calle de la Estafeta as if they own it. And there is something so efficient and predictable about how they gallop in a tight wedge formation of curved horns, as if they've rehearsed this and are trained for it. They too seem excited, except that charging forces them to keep their heads low which gives them a businesslike air, of needing to get a job done. Their taller rear legs give them an advantage over humans on this uphill course. Lagging behind come steers with their clanging bells.

All six bulls who will fight this afternoon are here, and the screams of the women in the balconies go up three octaves. The men, running flat out, get an additional spurt of energy.

When the bulls rumble underneath us, I bend in half, craning to get a bird's-eye view as they pass underneath. Maruja does the same, squashing me, cutting off my epiglottis, my sternum.

Rope ladders hang from all the windows. At the corner at the top of the street where the bulls are headed the last runners leap for cover. This is the first police barrier they can reach for safety. Some vault over head first, others sprawl on the ground under the bottom tier of the barrier. The bulls skid and turn. One stops and faces the barrier, but the steers with their heavy dalang-dalang bells bring him back to reason and drag him in their wake; he soon overtakes them and rejoins the bulls.

It's over in twenty seconds.

Maruja unclasps her white knuckles from the balcony, and I slowly breathe in for the first time since the last *cohete*.

'*Te gustó, niño?*'

'*Sí.*'

'*Gracias a Dios que no hubo heridos.*'

During breakfast, the old crone and Maruja discuss various miracle weight-loss cures: steel bands you wrap around your body, a gentle vibrator you lie down on, surgery on the stomach, and unregistered unapproved homeopathic slimming techniques.

Maruja suspects they are all tricks to get her money. By the time we finish breakfast, the street is back to its normal traffic. We return through the northern city gate, down the same street the bulls ran, past their corral outside the city wall. The car traffic obliterates all memory of this as a street of ritualized manhood and bravery.

The following morning, at 6.15 am, Maruja and I board a bus outside her high-rise on the northern outskirts of town. Maruja still has sleep sand in her eyes. She does not even bother putting her shoes on properly; instead she wears them like slippers with the back caving in under her heels.

'*Vente, niño, se nos hace tarde, vente!*'

We rush to the bullring and sit on the cement seats. At this hour entrance is cheap and the sitting free. Maruja forgets to bring the plastic cushions she set aside.

'You're the one with the skinny backside,' she says, looking through her bag for something she can use. 'You need padding.'

'I don't mind,' I say, staring at Maruja's ample rear end, and for some reason I think of those buttocks pressing down on the soft rubber toilet seat and how that seat must suffer whenever she goes to the bathroom.

'Here, at least take this old newspaper so you stay clean.'

'I'll get newsprint all over me.'

'*Estate quieto, y callate, niño!*'

Maruja is so excited and happy to be here, she keeps kissing me. The walk up the steep steps has left her out of breath and all red in the face. The stands are full of women and children.

'No, no, he has seen this before. The *niño* is just eight!'

Maruja likes to talk to her neighbours. Within five minutes they know my name and that I live in Paris and that Maruja and Manolo have been working for us for four years.

'If there is any bloodshed I will cover your eyes, OK?'

I know these idle threats are meant more for her new friends in the grandstand than for me.

When the second *cohete* goes off, the ring opens. Police at the ringside prevent members of the audience from going down into the ring or into the safety barriers.

Some runners enter. They are here so early, Maruja boos them. But after a minute or so of tense waiting, the flow of runners becomes steady. They keep churning in through that dark red chute (*callejón*) as if it were a giant sausage-machine and the flow an endless link of humanity. No one questions why so many young men are willing to risk their lives. Suddenly the runners come bunched closer together.

The screams of women in the bullring announce the bulls. Their screaming is part of the air, part of the morning. It is embedded in my scalp. Although there is nothing to hide, Maruja covers my eyes.

The fast flow of runners speeds up again. They are emerging into the ring at such speed that as soon as they feed out of the *callejón*, instead of running straight, they turn immediately left and right for cover. Now Pamplonicos, not tourists as before, splash on all sides, throwing themselves on the sandy ground.

This is the place where the worst accidents occur. The wooden entrance into the bullring is so narrow, like the funnel of a wine-press, that one runner tripping and falling can trigger a pile-up of humanity which bulls, in order to pass, must trample over or charge into.

I can't see or hear anything. When the first bull appears I know it only from the sight of Maruja's little feet jumping up and down in her broken shoes. The smells around me of early morning coffee and bad breath dissipate. Women stand up screaming in anticipation.

'*Dos, tres, cuatro* . . .' She is counting the bulls. They make it to the corral on the other side of the ring. '*Cinco.*'

Maruja's hands are pinching my neck.

'*Aie, aie, aie, donde está el sexto?*'

The sixth has not appeared, which is a bad sign. A bull on its own is much more likely to stop charging, turn, and gore. The dalang-dalanging cowbells of the steers break the tension, and they enter the ring with the last bull in their midst. Professional attendants, *vaqueros*, in black pants with silly red woollen hats and long wooden poles, run in behind the steers. Dalang-dalanging, the steers go trotting through the crowd and disappear into the holding pen on the other side of the ring.

'*Muy bien hecho, muy bien!* Perfect!' says Maruja, clapping along with everyone else.

Now the light entertainment portion starts, and the police allow youngsters from the stands to leap over the safety barriers into the ring. Dozens of scruffy street kids leap into the ring.

'You want to go, *niño?*'

'—'

'Go, if you want.'

I stay pressed next to Maruja's warm side. Even the small bulls look terrifying to me.

'Don't be afraid, this is for fun!'

A *novillo* or yearling has been let loose into the ring. It is about half the size of the earlier three-year bulls, but their horns have rounded cork bumpers placed on the end.

'*Niño*, don't be scared, it is not dangerous, watch. *Aie aie aie!*' She screams with laughter as a boy gets tossed ten feet up in the air.

The packed mass of runners opens up; people leaping on all sides give the horns a clear run. As soon as a *novillo* turns his head in one direction, the dense crowd separates and a long empty vista, a corridor of clean sun-bright yellow sand, opens up for him to charge down. It is fantastic to watch these endlessly formed and re-formed empty corridors. A living, shifting kaleidoscope. But the bull grows tired and ineffective in this exitless situation. Soon he seems rather pathetic and confused as the runners grow increasingly bold and taunt him, pull his tail, yank at his horns.

The derision and indignities they inflict on the poor yearling make me feel sorry for him. The stands start whistling their displeasure. It is not fair how quickly these proud and noble animals are turned from feared killers into objects of derision. At last a steer is sent out, dalang-dalanging around the far edge of the ring, collects the young bull and trots him through the mass of boys, back to safety.

Yearlings are let loose one by one, and they butt young men up in the air. Maruja's *aie-aies* have several decibels less cutting sharpness than with the full-grown bulls.

She laughs. 'That poor boy hurt himself.'

The young man tossed up in the air gets up off the sand and keeps running. But even so Maruja has tears built up inside her since the first *cohete*, and she catches them in her hand and dries her hand on my hair.

'Don't you want to go down there?'

'—'

'Look at the clowns and the midgets! They're not scared.'

The tiny clowns always make me laugh. They roll inside a barrel, trip in front of the bull, do somersaults on his back.

'Come on, *niño*, don't be scared.'

Fear which was just a little acorn in my chest has grown as big and hard as a bowling ball. I can hardly swallow.

'OK, OK, I won't force you.'

Maruja wants me to go, she would go down herself, I know it, if she could run, but I disappoint her, I don't dare it.

By the time we leave the ring at 8 am, professional photographers have already developed their black-and-white film of the morning's run and are hanging up their blow-ups for sale on large wooden stands.

San Fermín has a large fairground on the outskirts of the city. Every afternoon after the bullfight, when Maruja goes home to soak her bruised feet in hot water and Epsom salts, Manolo and I head there for an evening of goofing off. The place is huge.

In the bumping cars, Manolo sits next to me holding the dashboard and the back of the seat, trying to wedge himself so as to cushion the bumps, and he keeps whispering in my ear, 'No, no, no, slow down, slow down, *despacito*.'

I don't aim for girls, I aim for the hot-shot *machos*, the ones with zits and greasy hair who I know will come gunning for us and slam us with a vengeance.

'No, no, no, *chaval*, don't be crazy. What are you doing?'

We are rammed from behind and almost immediately from the side. The teenagers are drunk, especially the *machos*, so they lean out of their cars, bopping each other with plastic hammers, with *botas*, with fists, their violence fed and cushioned by drunkenness. Manolo winces and rubs his knee.

'You are so bad, so bad, *niño*, I don't know how you became so bad!'

I am on purpose driving counter-trafficwise looking for thugs, and Manolo is not enjoying himself. He lunges for the wheel, but it is too late. In grabbing the wheel, he has to let go of his wedged position, and when a car slams us, Manolo swears under his breath and massages his ribs. On the next go-around, he gets out and watches me from the sidelines.

Alone, I avoid hitting anyone. And I wave at Manolo to show him how easy and painless it all is.

My second favourite pastime is a shooting gallery, a tiny booth, always empty, on the edge of the grounds, but its air-guns are not too heavy for me. I cock one, load a metal pellet, and resting my elbows on the counter, I take aim along the skewed sights. I shoot balls off a small white wrought-iron tree. I come here so often, I learn to correct for the guns' deviation. Three pellets cost a *duro*. For five *duros* I can shoot down all nine white balls on the tree and earn five points or a plastic helicopter wing with a rubber band, the kind you wind up and which rises up ten feet in the air.

All week long, I collect points. For four hundred and forty-five points I can win the top prize, a miniature wooden wine cask with tiny copper-plated wooden mugs. I have my eyes set on that wine cask.

Manolo keeps handing the booth operator *duros* with admirable patience. This souvenir will cost him a fortune, but at least I am quiet and keep busy.

CHAPTER SEVEN

Joaquín's down and dirty,
real 'cutre' tapas bars

I do my remedial summer school maths correspondence course at the kitchen table. Maruja leaves me alone in the kitchen with my textbooks and the short greasy stub pencil she uses for shopping lists. I keep looking up, staring out of the window at the bastard's hut in the distance, his junk-yard, the lizard road baking in the sun. I loathe being indoors. Butterflies alight on the windowsill and fly out again. Maruja enters, leans over my shoulder and studies my geometry.

'Good, good,' she says, taking my tic-tac-toe doodles for worksheet answers. The window is open about fifteen centimetres. I can see something glinting in the distance. A pocket mirror? A waterfall? To lend encouragement, Maruja uses her butcher's knife to sharpen my pencil down another centimetre. This is torture.

The phone rings. 'Sí, sí, Señora Novoa.' I hear Maruja shifting into her polite underclass voice.

It is my Aunt Isabel, calling from Madrid. I say I am

too busy to talk and slice my index finger at my throat to let Maruja know how I feel about this interruption. I ignore these repeated telephone calls, push them off as far as I can, to the end of the summer vacation. But I know that my aunt, who has profited so handsomely from my mother's reckless invitations to our house in Paris, is going to make me pay the unenviable price of a Madrid 'reimbursement'.

Every time the phone rings I cringe, knowing it is Aunt Isabel meddling from afar, pulling strings to ruin my happiness. One day I make the mistake of answering the phone myself.

'Alfonsito, daaaaarling, how are you?' (I stare with longing at my geometry.) 'How is your summer going? I have been so concerned about you. I do hope that little fat woman who cooked so divinely for us the last time we were in Paris is taking good care of you? Is she making you nice *béchamel* sauce? Oh, I am so jealous! How does your mother stay so thin?'

It is harder for Maruja to ignore this aunt than it is for me, and they begin planning my visit to Madrid almost from the day we arrive in Pamplona. I try to limit the side-trip to the shortest possible time, but I know the visit is inevitable.

Maruja's short round stature is made even smaller, more dwarf-like, in Madrid. Her uncertainty about which bus to take, and how to cross the wide boulevards, translates itself to me. We feel like hicks trying to cross these vast arteries full of snarling traffic. The Manzanares is low this summer because of the drought, and the entire capital smells of raw sewage.

From the central train station we walk over to my Uncle Alfonso's office. He is a supervising architect for the city of Madrid. We see him at his large desk, signing letters, surrounded by a rush of secretaries. After a few minutes he looks up, seems disappointed to have to leave his office so soon, gets up, shakes hands with Manolo, and kisses Maruja and me. He is so tall, he kisses the crown of my head.

My Aunt Isabel does not know how to drive and uses my uncle as a glorified chauffeur. Except for the fact that he drives a tiny Seat, Alfonso, with his long straight nose, tall forehead and white hair swept back, looks like a king, someone who gives speeches and belongs in a palace. He was meant to drive us to his home, but tonight there is a family crisis, and instead he drives us to the hospital. We wait in the visitors' room, not daring to ask too many questions.

Alfonso's brother, Uncle Paco, rushes by us to see his only son, who has been operated for a benign brain tumour. Paco's wife passes us in a clinking and clanking of gold jewellery. Her long black gown, billowing out behind her in the white light, belongs in a remake of *Gone with the Wind*.

I don't like seeing Maruja and Manolo in Madrid –

among the Novoas they lose their edge of brilliance and laughter and retreat into being just another odd couple, a fat peasant woman and her shy gofer. We stand in the hallway, waiting to be told what to do.

My three Novoa uncles are tall, handsome brothers who in their youth were known for turning Vigo upside down, bachelors who won all the tennis championships in the province of Galicia, and even some national tournaments. For decades they were the admiration of eligible society women in Vigo. Even when I meet them in their late sixties and seventies, they are still ladies' men, and there is still much family talk concerning their escapades and how sad they made many a maiden. Rumours abound that they continue to break hearts.

Joaquín the eldest, lives in Vigo and is some sort of shipping agent, port captain and/or foreign trade impresario. It is not clear what he does, but everyone in town respects him, and Joaquín does little except sit around the country club, look handsome all day and call colleagues by their distinguished titles.

The two younger brothers, Alfonso and Paco, live in Madrid. Paco, a nuclear engineer, is considered by many in the family to be its genius, its best tennis player, and in his day the biggest womanizer. I never get to know Paco well. This evening he rushes by again without stopping to say hello. This is the last time I see him, hurrying to catch up with his sobbing wife.

★

Because all my aunts are holding a vigil at the emergency ward for Paco's son, Uncle Joaquín, who is visiting Madrid, takes Maruja, Manolo and me out to dinner. And because we have not made reservations anywhere, he decides to take us for *tapas*.

Our first stop is El Círculo de Bellas Artes. This is a dusty old art school, and only Joaquín's associate club membership here allows us into the large stately café area. Maruja, Manolo and I follow him in, under the high vaulted art deco ceiling. This is a haunt of the literary intelligentsia, a place where you cannot stand at the bar, but have to wait to be seated in huge overstuffed armchairs. The kind of neo-pretentious place I know Maruja loves and Manolo can't stand.

After a slow, somewhat stuffy start, we move on to grungier places. As we enter a nearby city bar, Joaquín explains the word *cutre*, a slang expression that implies more than the vulgar or the run-down, it means a vulgarity that is charming, a sort of glorified ugliness. Unlike kitsch or camp, *cutre* is not overdone or baroque, but provocative by virtue of its ordinariness. The age-old tradition of eating *tapas*, for instance, in dingy bars is suddenly chic.

At first, my reaction is that he is trying to hide the fact that he does not want to spring for an expensive meal, but soon I fall into the rhythm of the venture. He takes us from bar to bar, ordering only the speciality of the house, and then we move on: we go from the crispy shrimp fried in salt and pepper of Los Gabrieles, to the fried sweetbreads in garlic and olive oil at Los Alemanes, to El Mesón del Pobre for pigs' ears in sauce, to El Abuelo for squid in its own ink, to Museo del Jamón where the dried cured ham is so good just the aroma alone feeds you. Here huge cured hams dangle from the ceiling, and Joaquín introduces us to five or six different flavours of ham. Maruja takes her food extremely seriously. In one bar she buys a bottle of the cook's special olive oil, in another she begs the recipe of the shrimp in garlic sauce.

'*Menudos* (bull tripe in garlic), hmmm, try this, *niño*. This you will like, it is not too strong. And oh, *por Dios*, these *langostinos envueltos* (crayfish wrapped in ham) are to die for! Just one more then I am finished. I must stop!'

Maruja is not hungry, but she can't help herself. She coyly lifts a *caracol en salsa* (snail in olive oil) on the end of a toothpick, as if the offhand manner in which you eat might reduce the overall intake of calories.

Our appearance must strike the barmen as funny. In each *tapas* bar Joaquín enters looking like the heir-apparent to the Spanish throne. Walking with his raincoat thrown like a cape over his shoulders, he is our tall genial debonair city guide. Then Manolo and Maruja follow. They stand quietly and wait for him to order. We eat standing up at the bar. Usually Joaquín lifts me up and sits me on the bar. No one questions my age or what I am doing out at this hour of the night. I drink out of Maruja's sherry glass or her beer glass – water seems to be unknown or illegal in places like this.

We rarely stay in one bar for more than a round of *tapas*. So it is a road show, choreographed, with Joaquín driving us all over town. We don't speak much on the way. But Joaquín is so tall and portly, his knees are bent up on either side of the steering wheel, and his head touches the padded roof. Why all the driving? Joaquín laughs. 'Because Madrid never stops, it is a permanent fiesta.'

It is easy to tell that life has not turned out exactly as Joaquín imagined it would as a young man. For one thing he is driving a car that barely fits around his girth. But lack of means does not affect his courtliness or charm. On the contrary, it gives him an edge of pathos, a special humanity which reminds me of those White Russians driving taxis in Paris whom my mother hired to tutor us.

Maruja loves the evening, she loves Joaquín showing us all the sights, and they leave all decisions up to him. They have never appeared to me more like provincial rubes. Maruja yawns.

'Madrid enviously looks at other European capitals for gaiety and fun,' says Uncle Joaquín, using an old roué boulevardier voice, 'and although Madrid thinks the rest of the world has bypassed it, as far as I can tell it is way ahead of them.'

At 1 am we find our way to the art deco bar El Museo Chicoté. Joaquín explains, 'Chicoté opened his doors in 1931 and catered to Ernest Hemingway, Ava Gardner, Frank Sinatra, Onassis.'

Maruja, with her hands crossed over her black pocketbook, looks around as if she has just crashed the King's birthday party at Versailles. Manolo assumes his ramrod butler stance. We look more like Joaquín's retinue, his pages and servants, than his family and friends. He buys another round.

'This is the hangout of government ministers. There is a passageway to a back room where high-class prostitutes flock.'

I've never seen Maruja quieter. She even forgets to wipe off the moustache left by her glass of sherry.

Chicoté's senior bartender is the legendary Don Antonio Romero García. A grey-haired gentleman in a grey flannel jacket and black tie, he started working here in 1940 at the age of thirteen, and Maruja immediately takes a liking to him. Here one does not order, says Joaquín, one tells Don Antonio one's mood. Maruja, who is starting to act a little tipsy, says, 'Well, I don't want to get drunk, but I would like to party. I have not been out in Madrid since my honeymoon.'

Don Antonio oversees a squad of bartenders and waiters, but he takes special care of Joaquín. He offers me all the maraschino cherries I can eat, and he even grants me the special dispensation of a glass of water. His mixed cocktails have a pink or almond green sheen. Manolo drinks his as if he were sipping from a chalice in a cathedral. Maruja downs hers so fast she gets a second one on the house.

After the sane and soft tones of Chicoté, and Don Antonio's calming influence, we are off again into the fray. The night becomes a whirlwind of crowded streets, *champa-ñerías*, cafés. Maruja must be drunk, because not once does she suggest that it is way past my bedtime. It is clear Joaquín is a far different man without his wife, and he too is caught up in an anarchic, liberating turmoil of eating, drinking and joke-telling.

Hmmm, what have we here? A magic show in a disco? Interesting. Walk to the next door . . . Ye gad, it's performance art from Berlin, quick, out . . . give me some air. Now Joaquín drags us to live jazz. OK, thanks, I feel better. Maruja fans herself with a plastic menu; she has a grin on her face from ear to ear. In one rock 'n' roll bar, the waitresses get up and dance *flamenco* on table-tops to the applause of the leather-jacketed crowd. The eclectic mishmash of the Madrid night washes over us like a flood. Manolo stares at the leather bikers as if they come from the moon, and they likewise at him, in his neat V-Wilson tie and his black jacket.

In every watering hole, Joaquín makes new friends. In Paris it is only the young smart set one sees out at these hours, but here the middle class, the noble class, the no class are out in the street. Joaquín explains:

'A typical Madrileño executive works until 9.30 pm, picks up an out-of-town work colleague at 10.30 pm, takes him to a restaurant for drinks, dinner, an after-dinner cocktail, drops him off at 2.30 am and is in bed by 3 am.'

'When does he wake up?' asks Maruja, who somewhere along has slipped into the familiar *tú* voice with him.

'7.30 am.'

'How does he do it?'

'Well, he takes a nap, not only after lunch, but a second nap after work, before going out for the evening.'

Because Manolo has not yet offered to do so, Maruja buys Joaquín a drink. If she were not several social classes beneath him and a full metre shorter than he, I could easily see Maruja and Joaquín as lovers.

'Madrileños don't read,' says Joaquín, downing a cognac. 'And why go to the theatre when you have the best theatre of the absurd right here in the streets. This is our Ionesco!'

In the car rides between *tapas* bars, Joaquín points out Madrid's 'neo-ugly charm', as he calls it. He has no use for the baroque turn-of-the-century central post office with its monumental rococo towers and belfries, nor the Bank of Spain building and the statue of Alfonso XII in the Retiro Park.

'That statue is ridiculous,' says Joaquín. 'It is pompous, ornate and overwrought. But it fits the spirit of *coutré*, doesn't it? This neo-ugliness makes a whole kitsch subculture.'

Maruja and Manolo nod, much too polite and too ignorant of architecture to argue with him.

'You tired, *niño*?'

'No,' I say, yawning.

It is burn-out time for Joaquín and his three pages. He drives us past discothèques where Madrileños *à la mode* are

84

lining up to get in. Castellana, the broad avenue that divides the city, has a kilometre-long traffic jam at 3 am. Manolo and Maruja stare out of the car window at the ostentatious discos and glitzy patrons as if we were driving through a wild animal theme park in which you are not allowed to get out unless you are a game warden. Some cars here are triple-parked. Young members of this dawn patrol are talking like troglodytes. We hear them scream, 'Hugga hugga, me want'em l-l-l-l-love!'

'In Madrid, there is everything except shame,' says Uncle Joaquín, stopping the car to admire a young woman who is fixing her bra.

'*Por Dios*, let's go home, *niño*,' says Maruja.

Young girls drive home on their Vespas. Drunken voices call out, '*Sereno!*' (night guard), impatient for the little old man who has the keys to their house.

We forget to hang the 'Do Not Disturb' sign outside our hotel room door, and the next morning, long after our wake-up call, the cleaning lady enters unannounced. Manolo pulls the blankets over his head. A second maid enters with a vacuum cleaner, not realizing that Manolo is there under his sheet, dying of shame.

Maruja sits up in bed and studies the room service menu. She is far too hung-over for anything but black coffee, but she wants the thrill of knowing all the dishes that are available, regardless of their price. The menu's real purpose here is to grant the luxury of indecision.

The novelty of having cleaning ladies actually waiting on her excites Maruja. She does not want them mistaking her for a *grande dame*. She tells them she is one of them, and yet she does not lift a finger to help them.

'We saw the town last night,' says Maruja, trying to explain our lethargy.

The first maid says, 'The nights here are getting more and more crazy, I don't know why Franco tolerates it. He is getting too old for his own good.'

The second one says, 'The world is not only for the glamorous, the ugly ones have to have success too.'

Now a room service waiter enters and joins the conversation. He says, 'I work all day, so I don't have the luxury of seeing that degenerate world, thank God.'

Maruja had planned an ambitious visit to the Prado museum today, but I am careful not to remind her of it. The room fills up with working-class heroes that make all the partying possible, and Maruja beams, feeling right at home among them. The fact that she lives and works in Paris gives her an edge which they of course acknowledge.

'Who has time to party like that?' asks the waiter. 'When I get home at night I barely have the strength to remove my undershirt before I fall into bed.'

'We're on vacation, and we wanted the *niño* to learn about *tapas*, real *tapas*.'

The first maid has finished dusting. She closes the curtains, turns the lights off and leaves saying, 'You all take a good siesta. That tradition will never change, no matter how modern or new-fangled we become.'

Maybe it's the result of the hotel treatment, but later that day Maruja goes around with her head slightly tilted back and, although she speaks heavily accented French, sprinkles her Spanish with Gallic neologisms.

'I could get used to hotels,' she says.

Manolo watches Uncle Alfonso pay for our hotel bill in pointed silence. High prices always put him in a bad mood, even when it is someone else paying.

CHAPTER EIGHT

Madrid lives

When we arrive that evening for our required meal with the Novoas of Madrid, there are two seats missing at the dinner table for Maruja and Manolo. Of course, Joaquín in his early morning grandeur insisted they come for dinner and forgot to tell his sister-in-law. This is a sore subject, because Aunt Isabel always expects Maruja to drop me off and just disappear.

'Maruja is more family than most family members.' I say this pointedly, but my aunt ignores the comment.

Alfonso spreads his arms wide and in his deep sonorous voice says, 'Of course we want Maruja and Manolo for dinner, we just didn't count right, that's all.'

Alfonso is far too big for this small apartment. His shock of white hair, his broad tall shoulders, tower over the dining-room, giving the impression of a giant imprisoned by Lilliputians. When he and his older brother Joaquín are in the same room, they squeeze out all the air for the rest of us.

We sit around the dining-room table, and because I am

Parisian my aunt studies my table manners to make certain nothing she serves offends me. When Maruja goes to the bathroom, she leans over. 'That little maid of yours is a darling, isn't she?'

'Her name is Maruja.'

'What sumptuous dinners she made for us! Would you like some wine?' Isabel studies the label. It is embossed and looks old, but she is delicate enough not to say how much it costs. 'Tell us if ours are as good as French wines.'

'I don't drink wine.'

'No, of course, but just taste it, tell me what you think.'

'My father drinks whisky, and my mother tea.'

'Well, we certainly had some superb wines in your house.'

'Maruja is our wine steward.'

My aunt half turns, giving Maruja a sideways *moue*. She has pouted and pursed her mouth into a finnicky expression of distaste for so many years that now her face does it on its own without her even knowing it.

'Yes, Maruja is the best *sommelier* in Paris.'

'And you, Manuel?' No one calls him Manuel except for border police checking his papers and my Aunt Isabel.

Manolo practises his giant tortoise of Patagonia disappearing act, pulling his neck into his shoulders and retreating so far into himself he could have become a stone effigy.

Sitting at my side like a street urchin, Maruja wipes the dregs of old white wine out of her glass with a napkin and holds up her glass. My aunt pours and waits for her verdict. Alfonso and Joaquín are busy eating, oblivious to the rest of us.

The two daughters, María and Teresa, are pretty, but have always (because of their mother) been suspect to me. During dinner we barely speak.

My uncles come from an anticlerical republican family, openly sympathetic to freemasonry and social democratic ideals. But politics has been taboo in Spain since the Civil War, and even discussions of daily news items are avoided in their households, though enough hints filter through the silence for me to understand that at heart my uncles are socialists. Their wives meet their political comments with obvious silence, and often at dinner you can hear chairs squeak and the silverware (brought as part of their dowry) scrape the plates while we children try to think of a new topic of conversation.

'And you enjoy living in Paris, do you?'

My aunt says 'Paris' the way heroines in nineteenth-century Russian novels stuck in Minsk say 'Moscow . . . oh, Moscow!'

I wolf down my meal without exhibiting any of the elegant Parisian style that my aunt expects.

Maruja is so quiet at my side, it throws me off – I am unused to her not controlling the conversation.

'Tell us what is happening in Paris these days.' My aunt smiles. 'Is it full of tourists?'

'There are strikes and riots. And it rains every day.'

'What shows have you seen?'

I wonder not for the first time how a man like Alfonso married her. Was he simply not paying attention? Was he too much in love not to stop and notice that *moue* of hers?

'Have you been to any good operas lately?'

Alfonso puts down his glass. 'Darling, the boy gets up in the morning, he has breakfast, he goes to school, he does his homework, he goes to sleep. Paris is like anywhere else.'

'But I know his mother takes him to shows,' says Isabel, her voice turning insistent.

In the living-room, the Novoas have the same wooden cabinet as Maruja. A staple of all good Spanish homes, these monstrously heavy armoires store the wedding gifts that are never used, dusty porcelain and china. My aunt makes a show of removing a small silver key and opening the central and side panels, trying to act (for Maruja's sake, for she has given up on me) as if she uses this armoire every day.

She sets down fancy coffee cups for everyone, the kind of glazed china (with pink and auburn flowers embossed on the handles) you see being sold in gas stations around Limoges.

'I don't drink coffee.'

'No? . . . Oh, yes, of course. Every time your mother comes here we have tea for her.'

My aunt searches through distant dusty cupboards and brews me a special cup of tea which I barely touch.

That evening I sleep on the couch in the living-room,

for my one required night in their Madrid apartment (so Aunt Isabel can report to my mother and use it as a phoney exchange against future visits to Paris).

After tooth-brushing and after Alfonso kisses everyone goodnight and turns off the lights, he leaves with Joaquín for an after-dinner stroll – the two brothers have an obvious genius for walking the boulevards and gabbing in cafés with friends.

I lie in bed staring at the ceiling. Then I hear little mouse feet. Teresa and María stand at my bedside and invite me to their room to translate their favourite 45s. They ask me to explain expressions like 'shoop-doo-wop' and 'bee-bop-beloo-bop-belop-bam-boom'. The Beatles require less explanation. We know their songs by heart and sing them word for word together, seated on the same bed: 'I wanna hold your haaa-haa-haaand'.

That night, for the first time, the thought of tiptoeing back into my cousins' rooms or of spying on them in the toilet crosses my mind. I shut my eyes and try to make this whole misbegotten Madrid night go away as fast as possible.

In later years when we become teenagers and discover we are roughly the same age, this shyness and timidity will grow into paralysing bashfulness, and far greater heroics will be necessary to overcome it. Our easy friendship will change radically. Then I will lie on this same couch, tossing and turning all night, praying for a good excuse to visit them in their room, talk and maybe hold their hand.

Or just look at them while they sleep, that would be enough. As they grow and fill out, María and Teresa become more beautiful, more rebellious. But for now they are exceedingly well-brought-up Catholic girls who wear white gloves and patent leather shoes to church on Sunday with their parents, and look indistinguishable one from the other.

I examine them the next morning, rushing into the bathroom, in their pyjamas, with sleep sand still stuck in their eyes, and their curly black hair spiralling around their narrow faces. They still have babyfat. They giggle at everything I say.

Maruja and Manolo come to pick me up after breakfast.

'Thank you, thank you, for visiting us, *cariño*,' says Aunt Isabel, at the door, kissing the air and careful not to touch me, for my hair still smells of turpentine from my tarring by the gypsy boys.

'And give my best to your mother; I will be writing her.' She waves, with that overly-sensitive mouth of hers twisting in a sign of apprehension and nerves.

'*Adiós, Señora Novoa.*' Maruja waves.

'And you, Manola darling, you know my door is always open to you and Manuel, you come see us whenever you want.'

'Yes, *señora*, of course.'

CHAPTER NINE

El Pasha

Uncle Joaquín towers above his black-clad, devoutly Catholic wife. Being the oldest of the three Novoa brothers, he has just retired and has time to spend with me. Joaquín is a man of many talents. When he arrives in Paris, my mother tells him my Scalextric cars do not work and could he repair them?

Always patient and polite, he sits down at the end of the long oak dining-room table and spreads out my electric toy set in front of him; then, with his ringed ham-like hands, the hands of a roué boulevardier, he starts examining my cars one by one, turning them over, squeezing the tyres. I feel so ashamed that for a moment I want to steal back my ailing toy and rush it to safety. It is so absurd of my mother to show him this. And embarrassing. I have taken it back to the store countless times. We even mailed it to the manufacturer in England and still it does not work. Well, it works, but unlike everyone else's set, my cars bump along haltingly like tired blind mice.

I don't have the courage to watch Joaquín wasting his

time. To imagine that this retired gigolo can do anything at all is an insult to me and the car set. Just looking at him, with his half-moon reading-glasses perched on the end of his nose, makes me ill! What good are his social charm and ways with women, his gift of the gab now?

'*Hombre*, which end of the transformer is the right one?'

The flush of shame is so hot on my face that even outside the apartment my hate for him soars.

At the end of the day, I do not even bother inquiring about Joaquín's lunatic attempts. And yet, finishing dinner, I walk morose towards the front of the house and hear an unmistakable noise: the sound of speeding cars, careening around the black plastic track. The cars are zooming like greased lightning.

'You are a genius, Uncle Joaquín.'

'No, no, a genius is something *sui generis*. You can be a genius at one period of your life and then later a *dumkopf*. That is what happened to me.'

'How did you do it?'

'Oh, it was nothing.'

'It hasn't worked for almost two years!'

'It was set on 110 instead of 220.'

'No wonder it came back from the manufacturer as sick as we sent it. It was on the wrong current all the time?'

'Yes.'

I feel embarrassed and stupid, and when I hug him it is with eternal gratitude and a determination not to judge people by their appearance. His strong cologne rubs into

my cheeks. He puts on his jaunty felt fedora and his coat
that he wears like a cape on his shoulders as if it were held
with velcro, and rolls a rice-paper cigarette. His first love is
going out for a stroll.

To adopt a child in France, Maruja and Manolo need a
civil marriage licence. So, ten years after the Catholic
church ceremony, they have another wedding at City Hall.

I am the best man, and also maid of honour. And
because Joaquín is in Paris, he joins us. All four of us troop
over to the *Mairie* of our *arrondissement*; Joaquín, with his
coat thrown over his shoulders and his black sunglasses,
could be a Sicilian mafia boss. He reminds me of those
large tankers at sea that take a few miles to turn around –
when he stops to look at the gold-laminated woodwork
and ceilings in the mayor's office, it is a whole procedure.
The entire room comes to a halt, and everyone looks up
with him.

Maruja is wearing one of my mother's much-altered
hand-me-down Chanel woollen suits. Manolo is in his
Sunday suit best. Joaquín, towering behind us like some
movie director overseeing our paltry roles, keeps inspecting
the high ceilings, the golden cherubs, the hand-painted
cornices and chandeliers.

The mayor, when he makes his entrance, is a short little
fellow about Maruja's height. He wears a red, white and
blue sash diagonally from right shoulder down to left hip.
He stands at his desk, but he could be seated. Maruja and

Manolo are seated. Joaquín and I are witnesses, but I am first witness.

'Mademoiselle María Pilar Castillo Uviña Oregón, do you take this man, Manolo Gonzalez, to be your lawfully wedded husband?'

Maruja is smiling, laughing. Manolo has to pinch her hand.

'*Oui, oui, sí.*'

'And Monsieur Manolo Gonzalez, do you take this Mademoiselle María Pilar etcetera to be your lawfully wedded wife?'

'*Oui.*'

'Then by the powers granted to me by the Fifth Republic, I pronounce you man and wife.'

The mayor keeps shaking Joaquín's hand as if he were someone extremely important. We walk out through the leafy courtyard. Back at the house, Mademoiselle Etcetera, as Maruja calls herself now, has invited all their friends. Other maids and butlers, and her niece Rosinia who is in Paris looking for seamstress work. I play rock records on the record-player for them.

When I visit with Joaquín and his family, Maruja drops me off and returns back to her village, Villagarcía de Arosa, which is only thirty kilometres up the coast from Vigo.

Slowly I grow to know him and enjoy his company. At first he is a rather distant mountain of ego, but there is something so charming and vulnerable in him that I start to like his ego.

Every afternoon Joaquín takes me down to the docks, and we walk past huge looming cargo ships, under steel cables and hawsers tied around massive stanchions that hold the sea and the land together. Everything here is oversized and lit up by anti-crime lights. The dinosaur-shaped steel hulls and the mountains of cargo waiting to be loaded have a science-fiction quality and give Joaquín's words mythic proportions. He tells me stories of his early days in shipping. As we pass and enter through doors marked with 'No Entry' signs, port guards lift their hats to him. All these panels and gates marked with skulls and crossbones know him, all these flags from Liberia, Panama and Mexico, all the transistor radios set to foreign stations, all these foreign sailors trying to talk Spanish to ladies of little virtue, they all confirm what I have long suspected, that Joaquín controls not only this city, but much of the civilized world.

He leads me back to the Royal Yacht Club, a place where he once reigned as tennis singles and doubles champ, and, until recently, as club president. He takes me to his favourite spot in the bar, a round table at the top of the shiny wood-panelled stairs from where he can control the widest view and cast a deliberate blasé handwave at any passing employee or member.

Like his brother Alfonso, he also is too big for any table, too big for any room he occupies. But unlike his brothers,

Joaquín has entered that phase, past his polished professional years, when he no longer has to justify the hours he spends doing nothing. He no longer has to make a pretence of fitting into a role. Now he wears his Homburg at a cocked angle. He is a man who has grown comfortable with his size and the space he occupies.

Or maybe he was always like this, with thinning hair slicked back, shiny white shoes, silk handkerchief stuffed into the breast pocket of his blue blazer, the one embossed with the yacht club's escutcheon. A man who has all the charm and confidence of a South American dictator in exile. He smells good, and with his round face and quince-shaped body, even the table, even the bar feels dwarfed by him. Every article of clothing on Joaquín is somehow not as big or as dignified as the man.

'Yes, I could set you up here in shipping, my friend. Or if you wanted to try restaurant and hotel work, you could start right here in the yacht club. Life is all a matter of having good connections.'

It's sort of flattering and weird to be sipping an *horchata* juice with an uncle who addresses me as an adult. I have never done this kind of thing before. He's charming me as if I were his new partner or his date – after a lifetime of charming people he can't help himself. But Joaquín could read me the menu for all I care, and I would enjoy his tone of voice, his relaxed bonhomie.

'The secret to success, *hombrecito*, is not to give anyone

too much importance, but just to let them know you are here.'

With his sunglasses perched on top of his head, movie-director style, he waves languidly at some club employee. It is clear Joaquín likes it just fine like this. The top floor of the club where we sit is decorated to resemble the top deck of a caravelle, with port and starboard lights and various club fanions flying from a mast.

'The important thing about travel that most people miss is not to reach a destination, but just to be going. To be on your way. In life, always act as if you were on a ship, *hombrecito*.'

As we sit, the sun begins to set. Below us stretches the port and beyond it the whole city of Vigo. The yacht club feels like some celestial ship about to float into the cloudless sky, with Joaquín as our captain and social director.

'You breathe that air? It comes all the way from America.'

Although we sit in semi-darkness he makes no move to get up or to join anyone. The overhead lights switch on in the tennis courts, and to see better Joaquín slips his sunglasses off the top of his head on to the bridge of his nose. He looks blind; in these shadows he could be Ray Charles's grandpa.

'You know what is odd about women?'

'—'

'It's not ·their clothes, their brains, their bones, what attracts us is only their surface. Like flowers.'

He waves at a blonde who appears downstairs. For a moment I am not sure whether the young girl who races up the long curving regal staircase to kiss him on the cheek is one of his son's girlfriends, or one of his.

'The amount of energy man has wasted, no, that is the wrong word, I should say *invested* in women, would be enough to power all the electric generators on earth.'

His son Paco is playing on court number one, and though he is club champion, his girlfriend says, 'Paco is not the province and national champion his father and uncles were.'

Joaquín waves away the compliment but accepts her flirtatious smile. 'My dear, today more people know which end of the racket to hold, that is all.'

When Paco saunters off the court, sweating, with a white towel around his neck, and kisses his girl, it is easy to see that the father's charm and way with women have been passed on to his progeny. Alone again, Joaquín lifts his sunglasses and rolls himself a rice-paper cigarette. Are his eyes red or am I dreaming this? As he smells his tobacco pouch, he says, 'No, you must always let the women court you, rather than vice versa. That is the only way to have the illusion of remaining in control, my friend.'

Like their father, who married late in life, his sons will play out their teenage romances for as long as possible. Right now they are tall and thin, but they too will become giants. One will be a doctor, another an engineer, another a pilot.

'You know, in this Catholic backwater of conservative Spain, what we are doing here, you and me, doing nothing, looking at pretty girls, is a valid political statement. We are subversives. The Franquistas don't control everything.'

Joaquín smokes, regally indifferent to the ash that falls on the shiny parquet. When he has finished his glass of *fino* (the driest of sherries) and his green olives, and said hello to everyone including the janitor, and there is no longer any excuse to stay, he asks, 'What time do you suppose it is? I always make a point of not knowing the time.'

He walks me back to his house, ignoring the traffic. 'Walking is one of the great unsung pleasures in life, Alfonsito – don't you drive if you can possibly avoid it.'

These Novoas live in a large ramshackle apartment at 13 Calle Luis Taboada in Vigo, an apartment that goes on for ever and ever, and where most days the front door is left unlocked.

'We are directly in front of the police station, nothing can happen here!' explains Joaquín.

I once mailed a thank you letter addressed, by mistake, to 'Joaquín Novoa, Vigo, Spain', and he kept the envelope folded in his wallet as proof of what he had said for years: 'Everyone knows me in this country.'

After dinner Joaquín and his wife retire to bed early, but their oldest son, Paco, pulls out a guitar and serenades me.

Po-rom-pom-pom.

Girlfriends are waiting to be taken to dance clubs and to yet another yacht club evening – for high society in Vigo is a restricted *chasse gardée* where everyone knows everyone, and it is important to be seen in the right places. But my cousins, the four older Novoa boys and their two younger sisters, fill the living-room with clapping and singing. It is really to introduce me to their favourite music, but it is also a way for the brothers to reaffirm their tightly-knit family bond.

Po-rom-pom-po-rom-pom-pero-pero.

Family break-up is already in the air. They are each going off to distant careers and schools, Sofia to America to study, Fernando to the Navy, Paco to become a doctor and get married, and the demands of girlfriends are becoming more intrusive. The likelihood of these siblings serenading me or each other ever again is exceedingly slim. They serenade the house as well. They tap their feet, clap, slam the rosewood guitar. And, staring wide-eyed, I can only admire and clap along. Sofia and María sit on the arms of my armchair, just as overwhelmed as I am.

With just one guitar, the Novoas of 13 Calle Luis Taboada fill the house with a sea-change of enthusiasm. These ballads are not *flamenco*, not rock, they're love songs. The music is more alive, more unhinged than any record could possibly capture.

It is Saturday evening, and I imagine the Novoa girl-friends are cooling their heels in their apartments, waiting for the Novoa boys who have a reputation for being cads, rakes, and bounders. The girlfriends are planning the fit they will throw, wording the ultimatum they will lay down. But they have not yet interrupted us with hysterics and cries of 'You don't care about me.' A perfect evening has not yet been ruined, because Uncle Joaquín, the genius behind all this, the one who retired early, has taken the phone off the hook. An act which anyone who knows him knows has political significance. So we sing on and on and on, courtesy of Joaquín, and imagine this evening will never end.

In later years I will see *flamenco* concerts that feature a gypsy family, grandmother, father, cousins, grandchildren, all on stage, and they will always remind me of when my Novoas set aside their bourgeois qualms, and on that night of nights sang the roof off the house, and the *Guardia Civil* in the police station across the way walked out into the middle of the street and clapped along and asked for more.

CHAPTER TEN

Ludivino the donkey, purple wine and dance night in Villagarcía de Arosa

Maruja comes from the seafront village of Villagarcía de Arosa, set on one of five bays north of Vigo which are famous for their rugged, raw beauty. 'The five bays are where God placed his fingers,' Maruja often says.

This area of Galicia is considered one of the poorest in Europe, and after Spain enters the EEC, the area will be declared an economically depressed zone and will qualify for emergency relief. But Spain is still some twenty years shy of EEC membership. And Maruja's village is about as far as one can get from the modern world and still be in Western Europe.

This wind-battered, rocky, gnarled coast is inhabited by big men in blue sweaters, hauling in nets of fish and lines of mussels. There are few tourists. When the fishing ships go out, there are nothing but women left in the villages. It is wild and grand and barren. Grey basalt cliffs falling into the sea, inhabited only by cormorants and Gaelic crosses.

The rest of the continent is listening to Beatles records

and experimenting with marijuana, but here on the few hardtop roads along the coast you see fishermen walking barefoot. They walk barefoot in their villages, barefoot in their towns. At a bus-stop Maruja asks a fisherman, 'Does walking like that hurt you?'

The man lifts up his foot and shows us his soles, deeply calloused and wide. 'Don't feel a thing.'

'How about in winter?'

'Don't like man-made shoes. The ones God made are better.'

Maruja's four older sisters live on separate farms. The sisters have faces like old shoe leather, about the same colour and consistency as the fishermen's feet. What few teeth they still have in their mouths are mostly gold. They speak a mixture of peasant grunts and Gallego, a patois that is close to Portuguese. We smile a lot at each other.

Maruja is the youngest of the five sisters. Josefa, the third sister, is a skinny woman who every morning rides out side-saddle on Ludivino, the ageing family donkey, and works all day in the fields. When she meets me, after a year's absence, she does not embrace me or shake my hand, but reaches down to grab my scrotum and give it a firm squeeze. She flashes her gold teeth at me; I don't know if it's an insult or a compliment. I am baffled and do my best to avoid her for the rest of the day. That night, on shortwave radio, I hear that the so-called scrotal handshake is practised in certain regions of New Guinea and the

Orinoco, which may well be, but in Galicia it is unique to Josefa, and she practises it out of sight of the other adults.

Antonio, her large hairy husband, is a sort of caveman whose favourite pastime is making wine and hanging out with his donkey. They live with their daughters Rosinia, eighteen, and María Josefa, five, a couple of hundred metres inland from the beach. They never go swimming, they don't know how to swim. They are only tanned on their hands and necks.

The farm is muddy and dirty beyond belief. They have a well, but no running water. The bottom half of the wooden doors stays shut to keep the barnyard animals out of the house, but otherwise animal and human quarters smell and look the same. The bare stone walls are painted white every year. The furniture is rough and hand-hewn by Antonio when he first married.

Maruja and Manolo earned enough in Paris to build themselves a two-storey house on the beach in front of Josefa's farm.

One night after dinner at Josefa's, when we are getting ready to go to sleep, horse riders appear with guitars. Young men wearing long black velvet capes with coloured ribbons tie their horses to a tree. They serenade Rosinia at her first-floor window. She is beautiful in the moonlight, black hair against her white cotton nightshirt, an innocence on her lips. It is easy to see why she is the village sweetheart. Maruja loves her, I love her. But how can she resist this courtly love? They are so pure, so idealized, these guitar notes at night, plaintive voices at her feet. Rosinia could lean out of her whitewashed walls and kiss one of the two guitarists, but Maruja explains that her admirer has sent these musicians on his behalf; he has still not declared himself. I prefer to think it is one of the two musicians disguising himself as an uninterested go-between. Rosinia smiles, not letting on.

I make the mistake of walking around the farmyard inspecting the animals in their various pens – ducks, pigs, chickens, goat. Everything is OK, but something is wrong. Scared, I move about with the back of my hand to my forehead because Manolo has told me about the toads who at night spit poison in your eye, and I am leery of stepping on a toad in the dark by mistake. I should be in bed, but I keep investigating. When I push open Ludivino's stable, Antonio waves me in, '*Entra, entra, niño!*'

The smell of donkey urine and stale sweat gags me.

'Close the door. You've come to the right place!'

I know I have made a mistake, but it is too late to escape. Antonio and his three companions are lying pros-trate on the hay, their faces the colour of liver. An over-whelming acrid smell emanates from the rotgut wine fermenting behind them. Now I understand why Ludivino looks so unsteady on his skinny legs, he spends all his nights breathing in these potent wine fumes. The oversized casks and barrels are lined up against the far wall, one on top of the other. The men are smoking and laughing, stretched out on feed bags thrown on the ground. One of the wine spigots above Antonio is dripping, tink-tink-tink, into a tin cup that hangs off its nozzle, and Antonio does not mind it splashing a little on to his hair.

A naked bulb hanging from the ceiling attempts to unclog the shadows, but manages only to shift them around and creates new shadows behind the barrels and behind Ludivino. Not certain what to do, I move slowly past the shaggy warm donkey who stands there pointing his *bemierded* backside at the men. I am hoping I can find a way to get out of here without having to do what I know my host will ask me to do, but I don't want to hurt their feelings.

'Want a taste? Have some!'

I shake my head, frightened.

'*Sí, hombre, sí.*'

'No, thank you ... I, I can hear Maruja calling me back.'

The mention of a woman telling me what to do elicits a slew of epithets and calls for me to stay and disregard the old bitch, the hag from hell. 'We are men here in Galicia, men.'

The air here is hot and sticky with vinegar. Antonio's mouth is dark purple, and when he opens it, I don't see his teeth. All the men's mouths are purple from the wine. When they grin, they look like Hieronymus Bosch toothless skulls.

'Come on, try this one, you'll like it, it's *muy* suave.'

Antonio holds up a wooden mug stained mauve. I

glance around for the saving presence of Maruja, Josefa or Rosinia, but there are no women here.

'This one isn't strong. We'll cut this old rotgut with a little water, don't you worry, *niño*.'

The men wait, staring at me to see what I am going to do next. I don't have the heart to disappoint them.

'Hey hey hey,' says an oldtimer. 'Is *tinto* in Paris as good as this? Your Bo-djo-lay? Hmm? Well, I will tell you the God's honest truth. This here in Galicia is pure red claret grape, and Santiago de Compostela himself drank it when he arrived on these shores straight from the crucifixion. In Paris, they mix the Bo-djo-lay with Algerian and German half-breeds, and it ends up not being wine, but a mushy adulterated soup.'

'León, you've never even seen a bottle of French plonk.'

'I don't need to drink shit to know what shit tastes like. No, *señor*, I don't touch the stuff, because I value my health too much, and my soul.'

'And it costs ten thousand *pesetas*, León!'

'Yes, yes! But idiots who have paid ten thousand *pesetas* a bottle say it is shit. And I believe them. Ask Ludivino. Is that right, you ass? He wouldn't even wash his hooves in Bo-djo-lay, isn't that right, you old sow you? And you, Niño Shortpants, don't you sip our wine. We are not in France here, this is not a country run by homosexuals. In Galicia, we are real men. Women don't tell us what to do. Never. So drink bottoms up or go back to Maruja, put on your diapers and leave us to our business.' They all laugh.

León empties the wine on the floor and pours in a new brew up to the brim. I accept the wooden cup.

'*Salud y pesetas, y tiempo para gastarlas.*'

The sodden wood of the goblet rebels against the rotgut, the wood sweats and squeaks in my hand. The other men nod their approval. Antonio whispers, 'Come on. Don't worry, it won't make you as dumb and ugly as we are, only a little.'

The only soul in this stable I respect at all is Ludivino, and he shifts his weight and pricks up his ears.

'Yes, yes, in one gulp, down the hatch!'

I lift it to my lips and drink. They start screaming with glee. Ludivino shifts his weight from one hoof to the other. The wine spills purple on my white shirt and my pants.

'*Sí, sí*, nicely done, *hombrecito!*'

Antonio picks me up off the hay and kisses me with his thick unshaved face gritting against my cheeks. The wine is so bitter my teeth hurt. I look around for a glass of water to clean my mouth out. I see on their faces that same ugly laugh I saw people give the midgets in the bullring, and I want to leave.

'Give him some more,' says León. 'Some *aguardiente!*'

'Let him taste our newest batch.'

'The first drink is always hardest, now it will be easier.'

I lean against Ludivino. The long-suffering donkey ignores the men, but is clearly unused to being petted because he keeps turning around to look at me. The men are tapping different casks, pouring out various mixtures, intent on making me taste years that are smoother or less bitter than the one I just had.

'He's French, he grew up on Bo–djo–lay. Ask him.'

My mouth feels pasty and gummy, puckered with tannin. Each new smell of wine makes me sicker. I sip now, which infuriates them, for it is a sign of femininity, but Antonio defends me, saying I am only eight, or nine or ten, and that he is going to get into trouble if he sends me home to Maruja drunk.

'This is culture,' shouts the drunkest of the four, León. 'We are teaching you Spain, niño. Put a couple of litres behind your throat and that will teach you, you sonofa-bitch, to live in Paris. Who the hell are you to come all the way here and *sip* our wine? Christ is a bit of God that we saw here on earth. He came down here and he gave us his blood. We don't need no Bo–djo Rouge. This wine is the Master's blood. If you want to meet Him, drink!' León's face leans up against mine.

'You'll get him drunk, watch out.'

'Look, the boy's gone all white.'

Antonio tells his friends to shut up, he kicks them into submission, and when he has the floor, when even Ludi-vino stops shifting around, he says, 'My vineyard is in fact the best in Spain. At the wine co-op they have to cut my stuff with water, and they strain out the tannin, active bacteria and floating debris, because my grapes have real muscle.'

They laugh. 'Antonio, stop talking such balls,' says one of the men who has not spoken yet, 'and ask the *niño* here to compare our *vino* with the very best Mous-ka-dette in the world.'

'Yes, tell us, *niño*.'

'It is better than Ka-ber-nay, isn't it?'

'Maybe . . .'

'And how about So-vinhao? Ka-ber-nay So-vinhao?'

I smile, trying not to disappoint them.

Standing next to Ludivino, smelling his good warm fur, patting his shaggy grey hair, I am overwhelmed with empathy for him. In this stable his quiet patience gives him an honour and a status I never imagined when I saw him in the fields being kicked and whipped and pulled along. A recalcitrant lazy ass has become a working-class hero, a living saint.

When at last I stumble out for fresh air, the walls of the farmyard are askew, and the stars spinning out of control. I sit down next to the sow. She is not in a good mood, because her piglets were taken to market last week, but she does not bother me. It is impossible to tell how long my visit in the manger lasted. I stare at a sky full of stars and satellites for a time, trying to think. After a while I stretch my arms out in a cross because that helps me to hold on to the earth. The universe is spinning so fast I expect to fall off at any moment.

'*Aie, aie, por Dios, no me digas!!!*'

Maruja screams for Manolo. He races out of the farm,

and with Rosinia's help they carry me back down the slippery, toad-infested path across the main road, by the beach. It is a two-hundred-metre walk to their house. I grasp Manolo's neck for fear that we will both go spinning off into the ozone and never come back.

Maruja shows me how to shove my finger down my throat and vomit. It comes up burning my nose and throat, burning like hell. My skin boils. The tartness of that black wine still coats my lungs. I bend over with the dry heaves.

In prior years Maruja used to remain fully dressed at the beach, but last month she and I spent half a day at Les Magasins Réunis, on the corner of Avenue des Ternes and Wagram, and she argued endlessly with the salesgirl, trying on various one-piece bathing suits. The girl kept looking at Maruja's bosom and wondering what size could possibly cover her width. It was absurd of Maruja to expect anything ready-to-wear might fit her, and I hid my shame, trying not to imagine Maruja moving about inside the changing-room.

Maruja would come back huffing and complaining of the new styles. 'No, no, those bikinis are a public menace. If anyone ever wore that in my village they would imprison her.'

I don't dare suggest we go home, because she has that manic insistent look on her face of seeing this task to the end. We both stare in the mirror. She searches my eyes for

114

any trace of irony or humour, and I force myself to remain poker-faced. I do not want to risk Maruja having one of her famous nervous breakdowns here in the store.

She finally selects a black-and-white-striped suit which to me makes her look like a sea cow, a walrus in prison garb.

But it works.

This summer Maruja is not shy about showing her body. She waddles to the water's edge and watches me swim out, screaming at me to be careful. The sea is cold and full of big jellyfish. The beach is just pebbles. But this is Maruja's territory, and her overwhelming love for it is quite contagious.

Manolo and I go digging for clams.

Proud of her bathing suit, Maruja drags us to the restaurant by the single hotel down at the end of the road. It's a place for weekend tourists from Vigo, but on weekdays we have it to ourselves. She orders shrimps, *almejas*, mussels and squid.

'Prices are a fifth of what they are in Paris,' she boasts every time she swallows a prawn. 'That would be five hundred francs at Prunier.' She talks in old francs, without the new two decimal points, because it impresses the waiter.

She points to the fishermen down at the water's edge selling their catch. 'These oysters literally jump into your mouth, they're so fresh – use a lot of lemon.'

It's been two days since my binge in Ludivino's stable,

but my head still feels thick, my thoughts haggard. How can Antonio drink that way every night and still carry on?

We eat outside under the almond trees. The waiters bring us *albóndigas* and little *risoles* baked with green lemons and sun-dried thyme. Everything here is cooked in earthenware pots and we drink wine out of earthenware jugs with long narrow spouts. Maruja acts so proprietary about Gallego cooking, it's almost as if she were the chef.

Her favourite appetizer is the fresh sardines *a la plancha*. These are served brittle and black-barred from the grill. They are so crisp you eat the entire sardine from head to tail. In between sardines Maruja dips slices of fleshy rich red Mediterranean tomatoes in olive oil and spoonfeeds me.

By the time the *paella* appears, served in the vast burnished iron pan in which it has been cooked, I am not at all hungry. And yet I know the meal is only getting started. This *paella* has green peas, cured fillet of pork (*lomo de cerdo*), red peppers, fresh clams, fresh baby shrimps, crayfish.

But Maruja orchestrates the meal like an opera conductor, and when our plates are piled high with *paella* she keeps leaning over to select briny olives and offer them to us as teasers.

'It is so unfair! The French put down our cooking as a succession of peasant dishes, but they are ignorant!'

Maruja's beloved olives have multiple colours – fresh Roman green, amber and clear, purple, rose – depending on their maturity. Some olives are lavender, others brown, others crocus yellow. I am shoving food in, but only because I don't want to let Maruja down. The waiters serve us more. The owner keeps coming over and asking, '*Como está mi familita?*' as if we were all his children. The *paella* is still there, still half filling the iron pan, sprinkled with fresh saffron; but the waiters have the practised eye, and they know when to bring us dessert, leaving our flans and fruit salads discreetly to the side where Maruja can extend an arm and play with our taste-buds.

She feeds me fresh dates from Elche, which are chestnut beige and sweet as candy. She feeds me slices of orange and yellow peach and best of all, though I can hardly get it down I am so full, a sweet quince cheese called *dulce de membrillo*, and *turron*, which is part nougat, part marzipan paste. We sit at the table like the glazed fruit piglets on our side dishes. Unable to move, defeated and victorious, Maruja beams and repeats, '*Come, niño, come.*'

But her orders to eat do not carry conviction. She too is paralysed by the weight of it all. She turns back to the salad we have still not touched, and, unable to eat, she brings up the sweet onions and the ripe tomatoes to my nose for a smell.

'Spain is God's country, *niño*. And Galicia is where good people get to go while they wait to go to heaven.'

The dazzling summer light bleeding into the craggy limestone at the edge of the beach and blanching the almond trees invites us to take a siesta. She pays and leaves a grandiloquent tip. The owner promises to have fresh squid and a fresh goat for us next time.

Maruja has *dulce de membrillo* stuck on every finger, she invites one of the stray dogs to lick them clean. 'These are surely the happiest hounds on the face of the earth!' she laughs.

This gustation is not an exception, not part of her promise to my mother to add ten kilos on to my bones. It is just a meal at the restaurant down the road.

The lone movie theatre in Villagarcía de Arosa plays old Elvis films. To get rid of us Maruja dispatches me and Manolo to see *GI Blues*. But also *Elvis in Hawaii*, *Elvis in Alaska*, *Elvis in Trouble*. One day Manolo and I leave the theatre, bleary-eyed as usual, and stand squinting in the bright white sunshine.

'That greasy Elvis look is out,' I explain. 'Now, to be cool, you have to wear your hair long and fluffy, just-washed like the new English groups.'

Manolo nods. He stands with his hands behind his back, leaning against the movie theatre, not eager to talk.

'Elvis is still pretty good, isn't he?' I say.

It is mid-afternoon in Villagarcía, and there is nothing happening, except an asthmatic truck going by and a few donkeys carrying loads of hay.

'You want to go visit Rosinia at her sewing job?' I ask. After our last movie, we went to see her supposedly to say hello, but really I just wanted to see her pretty face again.

'See that, that is what will happen to you if you keep pulling yourself.'

Manolo points to a bitch that is being chased by a pack of horny mutts. They are all trying to hump her at the same time and raising a cloud of dust in the street.

We stand on the corner for a while, right under the marquee. We both still have Elvis's sexy smile and big white teeth gleaming in our minds. We stand here like a couple of bums with nothing to do and nowhere to go. I know that for Manolo this is special. Absolute freedom. He can do anything, go anywhere, and his wife won't yell at him, she won't even know. So we stand here, neither one of us wanting to point out our obvious fear and malaise at all this freedom thrust upon us. How far will we go in playing hookey?

Manolo has never once voiced a preference to me about what he wants to do. He does not smoke or drink. His main concern in life is to get away from Maruja's screaming and not to have anyone telling him what to do. Maybe that is why he stands against this building, watching the sunlight settle on the dust in the road. He is waiting for me to decide what we will do.

We can't stand here all day.

We walk around town. He lets me lead him. We sit and stare at the fishermen in the port pulling up their large nets. Manolo buys me an ice-cream. Sometimes I think Manolo married because he did not know what else to do with his life. Without Maruja filling up our afternoon, there is an odd crashing silence all around us, a terrible void.

Manolo never reads a book or a newspaper. I have never heard him suggest a visit to a museum or a zoo. His greatest pleasure is making up stories. Telling tall tales is his revenge against a world that bores him and does not appreciate him. He starts talking about how dogs knot together when they mate.

'And *niño*, if you are not careful that can happen to you. When I worked in a hospital, the emergency services were always bringing in couples who had got stuck making love. And then the doctors had to cut it off to liberate the man, and try to sew it back on later. Sometimes we just had to pull on it as hard as possible, and it would come off. Then you should have heard the man scream. The screams were terrible.'

'I don't believe you.'

'Well, you see those dogs, don't you?'

'Yes.'

'Well, it's taken them about ten minutes to become unknotted. But with humans it can take hours.'

Manolo never removes his shirt or pants in public. I often wonder if Maruja's outgoing exhibitionist nature is not a wilful counterweight to his shyness. Here on the beach, he stays under a big straw hat, sweating, trying not to be embarrassed by Maruja's screams and calls of, '*Venga, venga,* the water is so good!' He finds the Atlantic always too cold.

He's as shy here as the day I saw him enter the rank stagnant canal chasing after my battery-operated power boat.

CHAPTER ELEVEN

Ronalda's hinterland

Maruja wants to visit her oldest sister, Ronalda. She asks me to accompany her, and I can't say no. Manolo stays behind to work on the second-floor apartment of their house, which they plan to rent out to tourists.

Antonio saddles Ludivino. This side-saddle, the one Josefa uses when she hauls potatoes or carrots to market, keeps slipping down each time Maruja tries getting on. Now, hoisted and pushed by Manolo, Josefa, Antonio, and Rosinia, with María Josefa and me acting as counterweight on the other side to maintain the saddle upright, she manages to get on, but there is a loud crack and the wood of the saddle splits down the middle.

It is decided that Maruja should ride bareback, with only a blanket under her held in place thanks to a huge girdle Antonio manages to strap on. How we shove Maruja up I won't describe because it will sound too disrespectful, but you can imagine it. Her weight deepens the donkey's sway-back and helps to ensure she can't fall or slip off.

We set off. Shaggy grey hair hangs off Ludivino in wisps like the never-trimmed beard of an old man. Maruja sways back and forth to his unhurried walk, holding a black umbrella to ward off the bright sun. She sits there like a round pastry overflowing its dish. A wicker picnic basket is tied to the back of her makeshift saddle. Her blue polka-dot dress, for she wants to look good for her sister, rises above her fat thighs.

We plod along the edge of a field. Rosinia leads Ludivino by his halter strap, and I bring up the rear. Maruja clasps the animal's mane, but it is Rosinia, holding the bit, who controls Ludivino's forward motion. Maruja laughs some-times out loud, sometimes to herself.

Repeatedly she begs Ludivino, 'Forgive me for my weight, I promise you will go to heaven for this.' Then as the path starts to climb, 'No, no, no, I am going to kill you, poor Ludivino! What did you do to deserve such a fate, my darling?'

'Don't be silly,' says Rosinia. 'The *burro* has carried much heavier loads than you. He has carried wine casks and olive oil barrels and even once a stove and a refrigerator all the way up.'

'Yes, but he was younger back then.'

'Maruja, I tell you this climb is nothing for him.'

'I'm trying not to breathe.'

'Look, if the *niño* wants to get on behind you, Ludivino can carry both of you easily.'

'No, no,' says Maruja, like some mad medieval queen

talking to herself. '*Aie por Dios*, poor Ludivino, please! You will go to heaven, my love, *seguro*, *seguro*.'

Ludivino is picking up his feet slower and slower. I watch his belly sag with every jolt, and his shaggy fetlock hair drag in the mud.

The farm has no road leading to it, only a dirt path up through Antonio's fields, and up the side of the mountain. In prior years Ronalda always came down to the sea, and the family had its reunion at Josefa's house. But now that Ronalda is bedridden and dying, it is this or nothing.

Tramping along the edge of Antonio's fields, I keep thinking of my cousins on the beach, Joaquín's daughters and Alfonso's daughters. I could be helping them with their English, chatting, inviting them to Paris, getting them to become my pen-pals instead of climbing into the hinterland.

I keep ducking and bending to avoid the burrs and branches on one side, the maize and wheat on the other. As the climb becomes steeper, the path turns to glutinous mud, and I lag behind to avoid the generous sprinkling of Ludivino's hooves which go splotch, splotch, splotch.

He has this habit of lifting each hoof and, before digging it back into the mud, shaking it sideways as if to clean it off, and wipe it in the air.

Splotch, splotch.

I hunt for my cloth sandal, which remains stuck at the bottom of a mud hole. Splotch! The suction is so loud and deep it sounds as if the earth has gas and is farting all around us, and our climb echoes up the mountainside.

Ludivino keeps plodding along, pulled and insulted by Rosinia, who has little patience with his moments of hesitation and sometimes finicky attitude. His long slow lashes sweep up and down, staring at the mud that is splattering Rosinia's legs, and where her skirt is caught in the crack of her buttocks.

Maruja begs me to take her place on Ludivino so I won't dirty my clothes. When she sees I have mud even on my eyebrows, she howls, '*Por Dios*, this can't be the main path to her house!'

'It is,' says Rosinia.

'I don't believe it. Do they use this path to go to market, to sell their crops, to buy seed?'

'Yes, of course,' Rosinia laughs. 'And you should have seen us taking Ronalda down to the hospital, it took four hours, the stretcher broke. Antonio ended up having to carry her on his back!'

'I just hope I get there in time.'

What Maruja means is that the doctors are not bothering with Ronalda any more. I've never seen anyone dead or dying before, and I am curious how I will react. Especially if we're too late.

Rosinia is carrying her shoes in one hand, but in pulling Ludivino up, she keeps slipping and falling. I scoot ahead and help her. Now we are both falling down. Maruja is holding her wicker basket in her arms so it won't get muddy.

'*Dios, Dios,*' she laughs, doing the sign of the cross. 'Now it will rain, and then we will really have problems.'

Ludivino, who accepts untold insults in silence, accepts a fraternity of drunken farmers crowding into his stable every night, boozing it up and insulting him, Ludivino who belongs in heaven as the original nativity ass, Ludivino the shaggy Spanish moss donkey, starts braying. His mad *eeeeeaaawws* echo down the mountain and along the coast. To give him a break, we stop and pick blackberries in the forest. My mistake is to be too close because, without any warning, Ludivino urinates. The forceful jet splashes me, but there is something generous and clean about this *force majeure* flooding the mud and streaming down the footpath like frothy beer.

Ronalda's farm makes Josefa's spread look like a palace. The house and surrounding sheds are built on a steep slope. It shares a phone with several other farms further up the mountain. The kitchen is so dark and smoky that even though it has started drizzling lightly, they prefer to sit outside. Everything on this farm looks as if it were dying – not just Ronalda.

For years now I have heard Maruja tell stories about Ronalda. When their father abandoned the family and their mother took sick, she worked herself to the bone keeping the five daughters together. Maruja calls her '*La Santa*'. The Saint kept the family fed and housed; she spent her teens going barefoot through Vigo washing, sewing and doing anything she could, including selling her ass on the port to American sailors.

Now the Saint's face is all swollen, and she lies there not

moving, barely talking, on a sort of wooden catafalque, the type on which American Indians drag their wounded.

Ronalda has most of her teeth missing and a kerchief tied on her head pirate-style. Maruja removes it and combs her stringy brown hair. Now and then Ronalda licks her lips and asks for some water. Her skin has big sun spots from working in the fields and is drawn tight over her bones. Maruja seems happy to sit at her side, holding her hand, and talking to the others in the family, but every now and then she kisses Ronalda's hand, or touches her cheek, and turns to repeat loudly to the Saint what has been said. The Saint nods but seems not too interested in anything. The others act as if she were not even there.

Maruja entertains them with stories about her life in Paris, about Manolo's shyness. She presents Ronalda with packages of coffee, chocolate and tea bought at Prisunic and a gold necklace. The contraband we lugged through Irún, and up and down countless staircases, finally gets distributed. Each package Maruja places in the Saint's hands, so she can palp it, smell it, and then Maruja passes it on to the husband, who passes it on to a daughter who places it in the kitchen. The Saint looks so wrinkled and aged, she could be Maruja's grandmother.

To think my Novoa cousins are drinking Coke, reading books, listening to music is maddening.

Even Rosinia, barefoot and covered in mud, seems overly dressed for this hinterland. Maruja explains in detail how Manolo and I bought two old tick-covered roosters, and how she killed them, plucked them and boiled them, and this elicits howls of laughter and approval from the gathering.

I move off to play by myself. There is no level space. As soon as I go five metres from the house, the mountain slopes down on three sides. To keep busy I play *boules*, using a white pebble for a *cochonnet* and bigger stones for *boules*. I throw the white pebble, and then aim the bigger ones as close as I can get. The hillside is full of rocks, and I don't imagine my playing like this will bother the land-scaping at all.

Because she has exhausted other topics of conversation, I overhear Maruja telling them about me, my remedial geometry, my tarring by the gypsy boys, how many languages I speak, how I fly across the Atlantic with my parents, and that in New York we live in a skyscraper. They all stare at me. They stare as if I were a Martian. I can feel their stares sticking to the side of my face. I wish Rosinia would come and play with me, but she has locked herself in the outhouse. I cannot understand why this dying woman is spending her last precious moments talking about me, a total stranger.

'Come here, come, *niño*,' Maruja calls out.

I refuse to acknowledge her calls and become a trained seal for her family. I keep moronically tossing my rocks – I who have never tossed *boules* in my life.

'He's not shy, he's never shy,' says Maruja to the Saint.

'He thinks nothing of getting on an aeroplane by himself and travelling around the world. Nothing scares him. Not even Antonio's strongest rotgut.'

Silent Ronalda, wrapped in a black blanket like a papoose, stares at me. It is nothing I have felt before, but fear of suddenly having Maruja stay here with her relatives envelops me. Fear of this place. Fear of being marooned with crazy people. Fear of poverty and ugliness. Fear I won't be like Manolo's King Canute who dies and thanks to homeopathic miracle cures returns to life again and again. Fear that Maruja and Manolo and everyone here, including Ludivino, Rosinia and I, will one day die, and not one of us will ever make it back.

A huge silence settles on the hillside while they contemplate me. I consider hiding with Ludivino and his flies, but it means skirting down around the house, closer to them, and they're still gazing at me. They're like black crows just sitting there – I wonder if they've ever seen themselves in a mirror.

Maruja calls to me with an offer of fresh *paella*, cheese and smoked ham, but I don't trust anything about this farm – not the glasses, not the plates. The air is clean, but even that is suspect to me. I keep throwing stones, hoping we will soon leave. It is inconceivable to me how all this shit and mud and poverty produced Maruja. How did such a smart woman emerge from this primordial ooze? How can she share the same genetic make-up as them? I am angry at her for talking about me for so long. I am angry at my own shyness, this sudden inability to melt into the scenery and adjust. There is a beautiful view of green hills, and Maruja's family is full of smiles, but the silences get longer and longer.

Ronalda is the first to lose interest in me, or perhaps she was never too concerned with my fate to begin with. I see her eyes follow the clouds, then close.

Maruja starts fretting about the Saint's blankets and sheets. That is a sure sign we are going home.

They invite us to come back real soon. Ronalda's husband has a hard grip on my wrist, and he keeps shaking my hand without letting go. He has a kind and gentle face, far handsomer and nobler than Antonio's. It's a face with bulging eyes and a big nose, full of human solidarity; he's a man who would never make me drink, never insult his donkey. A boyish soul. But I don't want to waste one more minute here, I yank my hand from his grip and turn to leave without saying any more goodbyes.

Maruja invites them all to visit us in Paris.

'Isn't that right, *niño*?'

'Yeah.'

'Soon, Ronalda, soon! I'll see you again, my love, my love, my beautiful Saint, my life, my love.'

I turn away so as not to have to watch Maruja's big polka-dotted blue ass bent over.

Our descent back to Josefa's is half fall, half mud glide. No one talks. Splotch, splotch, splotch. From time to time I see Maruja wipe her face with the palm of her hand and flatten her cheeks. The tip of her nose is red. When we reach a particularly steep section, she cries out, '*Aie aie aie!*'

Rosinia and I assume she is slipping off Ludivino, but Maruja waves us away.

'I didn't want to say goodbye . . . I should stay at her side, should bring her to Paris. Did you see how beautiful Ronalda was in spite of all those pain-killers bloating her? Did you see how heroic and fantastic she was? The poor thing. She can't even move, but she never complained once. Not once. They will keep her there until the end, because she loves that farm, she loves those pigs. Poor thing, she worked all her life like a dog. Who needs money, if you're not healthy and loved by your family?'

Rosinia and I don't speak. We lead our tired queen down the mountain. She reminds me of the daughter of Ferdinand and Isabel, Mad Joan (Juana la Loca), who rode around Castile carrying the corpse of Philip the Beautiful (El Hermoso), her husband, bewailing his death.

Maruja gave the Saint her parasol, but now the sun is already setting behind the crest of a ridge. Ludivino is happy to be going home, no longer do his hooves hesitate and wiggle before plunging into mud.

Night falls before we are half-way down. And the stars come out. It is difficult going. But the full moon lights the landscape silver all the way to the sea. Rosinia keeps warning me not to step on any poisoned toads, or they will blind me. If she is joking, this is one of the best-orchestrated lies in the world, for everyone in Galicia tells me the same.

We pick our way out among the shadows like thieves. It is difficult to walk in the mud at night trying to avoid the anger of deadly bullfrogs. Way out at sea, I can make out the red lights of boats leaving the harbour of Villagarcía de Arosa. It is a calm cobalt black ocean alive with lunar reflections. Ludivino is too tired and hungry to balk at his load.

'You know,' says Maruja, talking into the void. 'All I beg God is that He let me grow old with Manolo, so that the two of us can use canes and hold each other when I have my white hair. That is all. I don't ask for money, or fame. All I want is to be allowed to be with Manolo. He can watch me grow wrinkles, and I can watch him become bald and paunchy. Wouldn't that be the most wonderful gift of all?'

Ludivino pricks his ears back. Dogs are running across the field to escort us the last few hundred metres into the farm. Maruja keeps talking to herself, while Rosinia shooshes the barking dogs.

'Ronalda is only forty-eight. Can you imagine? She looks a hundred and forty-eight. No, no, it is so unfair! Too fast. Too fast. Just yesterday she was raising me. Begging in the streets, selling her ass. She was so pretty, all the sailors wanted her. She'd come back with dollar bills slipped into her bra and her undies. The poor thing. She fed us all with that skinny ass of hers. What Ronalda would not do for us! And now she has five children. Why? Why not take me? I have no kids!'

Antonio appears unsteady on his legs at the threshold of Ludivino's stable. He waves. 'I thought you were lost for sure . . . I went looking for you. Josefa thought the wolf-man ate you. How did it go?'

Maruja does not answer. Her legs and rear are terribly sore. It is the last time she sees the Saint, her stand-in mother.

CHAPTER TWELVE

Pretty cousins all in a row: the Fab Four

The two youngest daughters of Uncle Alfonso and the two of Uncle Joaquín are my age, more or less.

Later, one will have children out of wedlock and become a graphic artist. Another will live in the US and marry a down-on-his-luck hippy social worker. A third will become one of Spain's new breed of liberated businesswomen. But for now the physical differences between them are minimal. I can tell them apart, but just barely. For years it mattered little which cousin was which, but now I am twelve, and things are suddenly different.

They grow long thin arms, cut their dark hair short, paint their dark eyelids blue and become beautiful. I manage to sort them out because two live in Madrid and two in Vigo, but when all four join us for a summer vacation in Maruja's house in Villagarcía, my life becomes precarious. This is compounded by the fact that their mothers don't trust the new American fad for bikinis, so all four wear one-piece black bathing suits.

I get along with all four. They each in turn go for long

walks down the empty beach with me and confide in me. I am the American cousin, and they want to come visit, they want to get to know me better.

Having grown up in a family of all boys and attending all-boy schools, I am not used to intimacy with females. I don't know when to laugh, when to talk. When is it all right to stop listening to their stories and to gaze at their long thin wrists, their flat bellies, their black loafers with little bows at the toes? Instinctively I figure I ought to choose one, show her more attention than the others, make her an official favourite because in trying to please them all, I will end up with none. But I can't make up my mind. And Manolo is no help.

'Take them all,' he advises.

'What do you mean?'

'Well, you pile them up and slip carbon paper in between each, so when you kiss the one on top, your lips will reach down to the ones underneath.'

'No, come on, what should I do?'

'Well, for starters, stop pulling on your weener, or it will fall off.' And he laughs his silent shoulder-raising laugh.

To buy time with the Marías, I take each one on long jellyfish hunts. They humour me.

Saturday evening, and we ride the bus eight kilometres into Villagarcía de Arosa. Manolo, Maruja, their niece María Josefa, and my cousins – the two Marías, Teresa and Sofia.

There is always a village dance on Saturday evening, which features a live brass band playing *boleros*, *jotas*, *paso-dobles*, fancy waltzes and generic oompapah music.

It is not clear to me why we go except that there is nothing else to do here at night, and we have been talking about it all week long. The dance is organized in a clearing off the side of the road and decorated with candle-lit red paper lanterns. The band occupies rickety wooden stands, and the dance floor is dusty bare dirt.

Manolo stands with me on the sidelines and tells me what to watch. My cousins look bored. No one asks them to dance, and they keep whispering to me how stupid everyone looks on the dance floor. In my short-sleeved shirt I have goose bumps up and down my arm, but the goose bumps grow the closer I stand to the two Marías. I agree with whatever they whisper. I can't take my eyes off their dark skin, their white dresses, their flat black shoes. If they wore high heels they would tower above me.

It is an unwritten law in these small Galician villages that, except for married couples, the men are too shy to ask the women to dance, and the few who try are rejected out of hand. Rosinia stands out because her skirt stops just at the knee – everyone else's extends half-way down the calf.

Rosinia dances with a girlfriend. Rosinia has a million-dollar smile, but she too is uninterested in anyone watching her. She is far too pretty for this village, these men don't deserve her. The less attractive dancers stare at the crowd of men, which is self-defeating because the bachelors seem to value only those who don't stare out, those are the ones they undress with their eyes. A few boys manage to entice girls to dance. I watch amazed, wondering how they conned the women into such a public display. Girls dancing together move in wonderful harmony and fluidity. But the heterosexual couples are awkward, the men make futile attempts to pull the women close and feel their thighs, breasts, haunches, while the women keep pushing the men off them. It's more a tug of war than dancing. A young greaser closes the distance, but his girl just stops dancing and walks away. Another girl who accepts the boy pressing against her breasts fights to keep his knees out from between her legs. This battling is far more fun for us on the sidelines than for the participants.

Manolo claims his nice bourgeois Basque upbringing is shocked by these peasant ways.

'*Niño*, don't look. All this will make you blind.'

I wonder how other boys learn about fornication, those who don't have a Manolo lying to them, driving them crazy? This can't be the optimum way to learn – all cockeyed – but I am not certain I would trade it for any other. Manolo has no interest in telling me the truth, and I prefer it that way, it keeps the game from getting boring.

Our coming here is nominally to act as Rosinia's chaperone because she is twenty-one and her parents do not want her going out alone. She wears flat ballet shoes like Marilyn Monroe and is clearly the queen of the dance. Maruja keeps urging her to elope with a boy: 'You will grow old, Rosinia, what are you saving yourself for? For the birds? Find a man while you are still young. Waiting will only make things more difficult. Look at me, look at what I ended up with.'

Rosinia blushes.

'Your ugly girlfriends will get married before you, then where will you be?'

I keep expecting to see her mystery admirer, the one who sent her the serenade; everyone wants to know who he is, but Rosinia is most discreet. We see no trace of him.

Up and down the avenue, all evening long, girls walk arm-in-arm in long phalanxes of bright sweaters and perfect hairdos. These defensive formations, brigades of giggles and whispering, ensure safety against rogue male pick-ups, and against village gossips, while letting bachelors know who is available for courtship. The parade of women seems endless. The arm-linked girls walking up and down the *rambla* take their promenading seriously, but Maruja has no patience for it.

'It is one of the few things these poor chickens are allowed to do without family censure. Some of them have been promenading for years, they'll die of old age, their virtue intact.'

Now and then a German couple takes to the dance floor – foreigners always attract inordinate attention – and then

Manolo and I grow silent, watching the couple link hips and groins, and do a circular grinding motion. Maruja laughs.

She keeps trying to drag me out for a spin, pointing to the prepubescents, five and six years old, who are knocking about, making fools of themselves among the forest of legs.

'Don't be shy, *niño*. When you were younger, nothing scared you.'

My cousin Sofía, who has been dancing by herself, looking so stern her jawbone could break stones, is joined by a young handsome farmer. He dances in front of her without touching her. The rest of the cousins gaze on in shock. Is she interested in him? Why does she not move away? Or say something? I marvel at her gall, impudence and courage – to do this in front of Maruja! I can sense that Tall María is jealous.

In my mind, I brand Sofía a hopeless slut and start fixating my desire on her.

Sunday morning, everyone sleeps late. The mussel platforms floating a hundred metres offshore look calm and quiet, foundations for high-rise apartment buildings that will never be built. At low tide women dig for clams.

I walk the wide sandy beach in search of Portuguese men-of-war. I am merciless in my hunt. I cut them to pieces and tear their long stinging tentacles with my long stick. There is nothing I hate worse than jellyfish, and this summer I have my work cut out for me. I gather them in a plastic bucket, and when the bucket is full I empty it out by the side of the road, leaving the jellyfish to dry out and rot in the sun.

I invite Tall María on a jellyfish hunt. She hates their stingers and approves of my ridding the beach of them. To remove her from Maruja and the prying eyes of the village gossips, I lead her all the way to the Falange camp, beyond the restaurant at the far end of the rich people's beach. I have never kissed a girl, but I keep imagining that if the two of us are alone for long enough something will happen. Since I don't know how to trigger a kiss, or even communicate my desire to Tall María, I keep walking at her side, often brushing up against her arms. I study her toes, her long legs, narrow hips.

The beach ends at a breakwater where reinforced concrete slabs meet barbed wire. We run into the dunes, drop down on our knees and examine the Falangist camp. The dune grass makes light imprints on her tanned forearms.

'*Mira*, María.' I point to the soldiers.

Some sort of ceremony is taking place in the central square between the barracks. A priest is blessing the flag of Spain and the regimental flags, and these are run up the flagpole. Colonels and majors salute. On three sides of the yard boys of my age in uniforms stand at attention. This is no ordinary boy-scout camp; each platoon in turn gives the Falange salute, right hand extended diagonally to the sky, the kind of salute you only see bad guys doing in Second

World War movies. Then the speakers crackle with music, and they sing the Falange anthem, 'Cara al Sol'. For a while they stand in total silence, their shoes shining, belts polished, fanions blowing in the wind. Some general is delivering a speech. We see his chest rise and fall taking deep breaths. Now and then the wind carries his words to us, *Dedication . . . Church! . . . Defence of the motherland*. Tall María and I hug the grass. Compared to them, I feel terribly decadent, barefoot in my swimming trunks, my thoughts focused on only one thing – Tall María. The air around us is impregnated with her skin cream.

They fire twelve volleys into the air. I use this as an excuse to put my hand on Tall María's back, to calm her, but I am the one who needs calming. She nuzzles her face into my neck.

'Alfonsito, make yourseif as small as possible. Hide.'

'You think they'll think . . . we're spies.'

'Maybe.'

'Maybe what?'

'They'll think we're making fun of them.'

It is incredible to me that in the age of the Beatles, they're still churning out little Hitlers.

'All this saluting and flags and uniforms are neat, I mean in a weird sort of way, don't you think?'

'Galicia is backward,' whispers Tall María. (I suspect her, with her Franquist mother, of saying this only to sound cool.)

'Fascists give me the creeps,' she says.

'Why?'

'Franco is old, and everyone says he will die soon, but it will take a century for things to change here.'

It is not a failed day – I have smelled and studied (she has let me) every centimetre of Tall María's visible portions. We are tight as thieves.

I get the idea of building a fort in the woods. And I ask my cousins to help me.

For a while all four serve me – Handmaiden from hell get me stick! Handmaiden fetch leaves and branches. Me Tarzan. Handmaiden, water! HM sweep the entrance of fort. Bring wood. Hold logs. Hold while I nail this in. Here, Tall María hold nail. Sofia hold clawhammer. Teresa hold prick – hold prick of bush away from me.

It is a grand performance. Having a master clawhammer gives me some much-needed authority, some natural selection. I remove my T-shirt. The Marías have no choice but to watch me sweat.

Of the four girls, the cousin with the most ladylike, most refined tastes, the one I would never imagine dirtying her knees or hands, Tall María, stands close by me and helps me the most. When an argument breaks out about the shape of the fort – One door? Two windows? Three doors? Don't you know anything? For quick escape, in case of attack or betrayal, we need manifold exits – Tall María takes my side. So does Teresa.

'You are doing a terrible job,' says Sofia. 'You've never

built a fort in the woods worth a damn and never will either.' She quits in disgust.

Tall María whispers to me, 'We are well rid of her.'

I smile, but am quite unnerved by her proximity, the smell of her warm skin, the speed with which she agrees to everything I say, always nodding, always smiling.

'Keep going, you are doing just fine, Alfonsito, I like your fort design a lot.'

At the end of the day the nailing, sweeping, brushing results in a space which requires an enormous amount of imagination to resemble a fort. But it is there. The beginnings of Versailles. The very beginnings.

Sweaty, tired and grimy with burrs and pine-needles, we return to Maruja's house. I am watching Tall María's pigeon-toed feet, delicate and suntanned, and cannot take my eyes off how sweetly she lifts her heels and puts them down in the soft sand. She has an hourglass waist and hips that barely move from side to side. When she stops to remove a pine-needle from her foot, she leans on my arm, and her bangs touch my skin. Studying her sole, she gets an itch and rubs her cheek on her wrist.

'Can you see if you can find where it went in?'

I kneel before her as she sits on a low wall. I search the long thin foot for any imperfection, any black dot. I force myself not to kiss her toes. With a pair of tweezers I squeeze out the splinter slowly. Twice she gasps in pain. When a drop of blood appears, I lick it, but she yanks her toes away.

'It was bleeding.'

'I'm sorry, no one ever did that to me before, Alfonsito, licked a wound.'

I taste her salty blood. Though we never use the word, Tall María is my first girlfriend.

Joaquín's wife takes the four girls and me to see the Beatles' movie, *A Hard Day's Night*. We feel silly being chaperoned by Aunt Conchita, but the Film Board has rated the Beatles unfit for unaccompanied minors, meaning anyone thirteen and under. Sofia is fourteen, but the two Marías are thirteen, and Teresa and I lag behind at twelve.

It is ridiculous to be accompanied to such a movie, especially when I am trying to have a girlfriend. In the darkness I sit between Teresa and Tall María.

Conchita is the most devout Catholic in the family. Thin as a rail and dressed all in black, there is nothing phoney about her. She could easily be the Grand Inquisitor. She attends chapel every morning. I do not mind her, because unlike other bourgeois aunts she makes no pretence of being interested in this world or even concerned by it. When the house is empty, I imagine her mouthing prayers or reading Saint Paul's epistles to the Philippians. There can be mounds of dust and sleeveless records lying all over the living-room, but Conchita will be praying and checking her holy water, blessed by the Pope – plastic crucifix-shaped bottles that she keeps in the back of a closet. Conchita is not of this world, except inasmuch as her family money allows Uncle Joaquín the luxury of playing the grand vizier in the Royal Yacht Club.

Conchita accompanies us to a matinée of the Beatles. It is the first afternoon showing, and we are the only ones in the theatre. She sits in the middle staring at the Fab Four as if they were something from the moon. In the dark my hand creeps over to Tall María on my right. I feel her long cool fingers. It is ludicrous to be doing this right under her mother's eye. After a while our palms grow moist, and there is something lewd and quite sexual about the moisture, but neither of us lets go. We know these songs by heart, every note, every word translated.

Dinero no puede comprar mi amor.

We lace every finger, then after a while I cup her hand in mine. When Conchita looks down at the floor, Tall María slips my hand under her left buttock. What is she doing? Tall María is already a lady, and I assume she is telling me to behave, or maybe she is giving me a feel of her cheeks? I wait for something to happen. I cannot concentrate on the screen. Only my peripheral vision is alive. And my hand squashed by her weight. I have never been here before.

Hysterical fans run screaming through a train station searching for the Fab Four. Teresa on my left touches my elbow again. It is the second time she's done it; the first time I thought she was just trying to make herself comfortable in her chair. Teresa is Conchita's youngest niece; at twelve she still has her babyfat. She has not started rebelling, never showed much of any personality. Teresa touches my arm and clasps my left hand. On the screen, the Fab Four are wearing moustaches and fake glasses to avoid detection.

If Tall María sees me flirting with Teresita, I am finished. I try relaxing and acting like none of this is important, but I cannot concentrate on the film.

The Fab Four go up to their hotel, they pull out different keys, say goodbye to each other and enter four different rooms, but when they close the doors they are all in one big connecting apartment. '*Hola*,' says George Harrison.

'*Hola chicos, qué pasa*,' says John Lennon.

'*Nada, y el que nada no se ahoga*,' says Ringo.

Only McCartney sounds at all plausible in Spanish.

We emerge from the theatre squinting in the bright garish sunlight. Conchita is smiling. She does not criticize the music; on the contrary she feigns to like it and even the Liverpudlian mop-top haircuts, but praise from her is the worst kind of indictment.

Walking home, Tall María is prim and proper. Having graced my hand with the firm weight of her buttocks, she now acts as if I do not exist. She does not even brush up against my short-sleeved arms. I treat this distance as proof of the secret bond that unites us. Teresa on the other hand follows me like a puppy. She is not subtle enough to catch my coldness.

At night when I sleep on the living-room couch, full of sleeveless Beatles records, when even the police station across the street turns off its lights, and all of Calle Luis Taboada is asleep, I dream of tiptoeing into Tall María's room and crawling into her bed. But in truth it could be Short María. Or Teresa. Or Sofia. Sometimes, in my madness, I imagine I should declare my amorousness to Sofia, the one who seems least interested in me, because her unsmiling face, her deep eyes are a definite come-on. Could her haughtiness be a type of desire? An attempt to attract me by her indifference?

CHAPTER THIRTEEN

End of summer flamenco blues

The movies shown this year in Villagarcía grow steadily worse. The theatre has no more Elvis films, and instead goes for old tearjerkers less conducive to flirting. Comedies in which a young nun speeds around on her trusted donkey to save churches and children – this is a sequel to the hugely successful *Ludivino, Pan y Vino*. Melodramas in which a nun dies and flies up to heaven, holding on to her wimple, while the bishop and the bellringer, who are both in love with her, cry.

Only the sound of salted sunflower *pipas* being cracked open and the tick-tick of spent shells falling to the ground provides any verisimilitude to real life in this theatre. The nun movies are so uncool, so retrograde, I feel embarrassed to be sitting watching them. Tall María is busy licking her crushed lemon ice, and I don't have the courage to put my hand on her thigh or kneecap. It's hot as hell, but María's skin smells lovely. My disappointment when the lights come on in the theatre is punctuated by a steady crunch-crunch as I follow her out on a bed of empty sunflower shells. We don't discuss the movie. For the rest of the summer, these flying nun movies put an end to our delicious interludes in the dark.

At dinner, during her parents' visit, I drop my knife, and when I pick it up under the table, I notice Tall María's knees are spread apart so I can see her panties. She widens her knees imperceptibly – does she do this knowing I am under the table? What should I do? What might be appropriate? For the rest of the meal, terrified of the madness coursing through my veins, I cannot look Uncle Joaquín in the eye.

It's the end of summer, and this is our last dinner at the restaurant on the end of the beach. Tonight, Maruja has prepared the *béchamel* sauce for the shark steak.

It is a Monday night and we have the place pretty much to ourselves. At Maruja's urging, the two Marías begin to dance and sing *flamenco* together. The waiters join in. The bartender breaks into soul-wrenching lyrics, accompanying himself with two small stemless wine-glasses held like castanets. Maruja calls Dieguito the bartender 'Byron' because he has written over five hundred poems over the years and keeps them all neatly stacked under the sink, by the cups and the glasses.

The two Marías go through a repertoire of *flamenco* songs, *sevillanas*, *tanguillos*, *zarzuelas*, *zorongos gitanos* and *malagueñas*. The owner stands behind Maruja, blinking and smoking his acrid black tobacco.

Byron is tall with slicked-back wavy hair, and he looks almost North African. When he sings he holds his left hand out, his whole body language is tense, the only movement coming from his hand and his upper body. His long-drawn-out *melismas* (similar to the sound a man makes when he is having a molar pulled) drive upward, fitful and pressing. His words are so distorted, so drawn-out, so unrecognizable, the guy could be on a minaret calling the faithful to prayer.

'It's the song of the Alley of the Seven Heads,' Maruja whispers, easy tears brimming in her eyes.

And maybe it is, but all I can make out of Byron's words is, 'I bought a new suit today, but the trousers are baggy.'

'He's made a bad choice in clothing,' whispers Manolo, who watches all this with critical silence.

Of course, the words are not meant to be taken literally; gypsies don't rant and rave every time they come back from the clothing store or when they go to buy a shirt. Byron's clothing problems are just an excuse for him to tell us the state of his soul (there are no smiles in *flamenco*, ever). Everything here is taken *seriously*, but not literally. What Byron conveys and what he means has nothing to do with his words.

'*Flamenco* is not a song, *niño*,' Maruja tells me, 'it is an atmosphere, a mood, that is why no one cares what the words say or do not say.' Maruja has no gypsy blood and has never danced *flamenco*, but that does not stop her from offering me lessons.

149

'*Niño*, to practise the movement of the arms you must imagine you are picking an imaginary pear out of the air. Go ahead, try it now, bring your hand to your mouth, take a bite out of the imaginary pear and then throw it away.'

With her small chubby hands and fingers bent at the middle knuckle, Maruja keeps demonstrating how it ought to be done. Her hands turn so much, they appear to dislocate at the wrist.

My cousins, who as far as I know only listen to the Beatles, the Animals and the Rolling Stones, are trying to show off; maybe they are slightly drunk. But suddenly they start a hard staccato hand-clapping, a *zapateado* while they turn and turn and turn in the mirror. The cook starts dancing with them. The dog howls. The grandfather of one of the waiters pulls out his wooden flute and plays, 'Poor Bartolo had a flute with only one hole'. Everyone joins in. This village is one big extended family. Maruja says, '*La calle es la vida, y el apartamento es un complemento*' (Life is in the streets, one's apartment is only incidental).

We've had dinner, and the kitchen is closed, and the lights have been doused, the front door closed just in case the police should be checking. But in the half-light thick with cigarette smoke, I notice that a few *tapas* have appeared, a goodbye gesture for Maruja.

We are crowded into the back bar where the noise is least likely to filter out into the street. Byron has brilliantine slipping off his thick jet-black hair, and as he sings his big hands grip the back of a chair. Judging by the way he stares at Rosinia, I can't help but imagine he is her secret admirer.

His song is a long, cigarette-hoarse, nasal, monotonous Moorish wailing that breaks and leaps out of his chest, punctuated by tight staccato clapping, and the two Marías' beautiful hand arabesques. Byron's wailing ends in a guttural hiccup and guitar notes spilling out and cascading all over the floor.

Maruja sits with her fat legs slung on the arms of a wicker chair, and she practises her hand arabesques.

The *zapateado* grows more intense. Tall María's toes and heels slap the floor in a virtuosic machine-gun subdivision of beats. I stare at her long calves, her knees, her hips. She holds her body rigid, her arm extended upward, stone-faced and austere, the fluid movement of her curled hand opening and closing as it turns in the air, bringing that imaginary pear down to her mouth and tossing it away. For Tall María, this is a goof, a joke, but I have never seen her more beautiful than tonight. All the waiters admire her.

The late night goodbye moves with long curving balletic arm gesture and a minute strumming, the guitar notes travelling up one's spine and down to one's nerve endings.

Galicia is one of the most conservative provinces in Spain – here the black-shawled crones hiss at girls who wear skirts that reveal their kneecaps – but tonight there is sex in the air: Tall María is wearing neon pink tights, and

Short María a harsh yellow and blue top. Teresa and Sofia each have long gold and coral earrings they bought from a gypsy.

In the middle of pouring me a glass of water, Teresa whispers, '*Mira.*' A beggar has appeared at the door. The man, not receiving anything, hurls this insult at the waiter, '*Vete a servir, sirviente!*' (Go serve, servant!)

I wish I were musical. The attack, the syncopation, the slow introduction, the ripping apart of syllables, as Byron sets the mood, and the Marías amplify it with their twirling, and the guitarists intensify it – I wish I knew how the whole energy of this music and of the evening is harnessed and drives to critical mass. But too much knowledge can be its own kind of ignorance. You don't want to be too insightful, too rational with *flamenco* or you'll miss this completely.

My parents have taken me to *flamenco* restaurants in Paris (where my big treat was to order bull testicles). I have spoken to countless performers at La Venta, between their acts. But outside Spain this music becomes a bit like a flower cut off at the roots. It becomes *a show*, with a beginning when you start your meal, a middle and an end when you pay and leave. But here, even in northern Galicia, *flamenco* is a way of life, and the music goes on all year, day in, day out. Scratch any Spaniard and not far under the surface you will find a frustrated *flamenco* wannabe.

'A balance between the dramatic and the virtuosic,'

whispers the owner, as if explaining what is unexplainable about Byron.

Motorbikes and motorcars go by, leaving the smell of old dust mingling with the aroma of petrol fumes. A large television in the hotel lobby room casts its blue light against the dancers.

Byron emerges from one of the back rooms with a green and yellow polka-dot fiesta dress – it has bouffant leg-of-mutton sleeves and five layers of petticoats. I am jealous to the core as he helps Tall María to step into it and zips her up the back.

With Tall María on stage, following Byron's beautiful heartrending melodies, and me impotent and on the sidelines, suddenly the number of admirers she will have when I am gone overwhelms me, the number of jokes they will tell her, the flowers they will offer her, the charm and cars and money and words of love they will throw at her feet. It all seems so hopeless, so enormously impossible, that I start hating the music, hating Byron, hating Tall María for being too beautiful, and too free with her laughter, too available to anyone who wants to have fun with her.

Byron has put on a black suit with tight pants. Tall María's wildly colourful outfit with its multi-layered skirts and tight bodice fits her as if it had been tailored for her.

Maruja whispers, '*Flamenco* is like a drug, it gets into your blood, *niño*, be careful.' Then she calls out encouragement to Byron, who is dancing step for step with María, holding his sweaty shirt closed with one hand tucked behind his belt, '*Así es señor, olé!*'

There is constant repartee between performer and audience. Maruja leads this give and take.

'Have you really lost your love?' shouts Maruja. 'Don't feel bad, another one, a better one will come along.'

We're mainlining rhythms and counter-rhythms. I succumb to the *fandango de huelva* – or is it a *rasgueado*, or a *granadina*? I harbour little hope of ever regaining Tall María, but I want to take her one last time to a deserted beach and there I will slit her throat.

'Camarón, Camarón!' They invoke the great *flamenco* singer, Camarón de la Isla, and the guitarists Paco de Lucia and Manitas de Plata, the way a baseball team might call upon the spirit of Babe Ruth, Mickey Mantle and Hank Aaron.

Aiie, aiie, aiie, aiie, aiie!

Maruja gets up, and the waiters move back to give her a wide berth. I expect the evening now to lapse into burlesque, but not at all – Maruja moves with surprising agility. She does not ooze sex like Tall María, but a toss of her hair, the flip of her wrist, tells you this potbellied woman was a killer not too long ago. She tries to make like a whirling dervish and her blouse pops its buttons, provoking screams from the cousins. The men holler for more. They love her size – this mass of flab and jelly moving and shaking is somehow so life-affirming, so imposing; they are transfixed by her. No one is laughing.

Tall María sits down at my side, panting and sweaty. She puts her hand on my back. I don't touch her, don't move close to her, but I wait for her fingers to caress my neck.

The tempo slows down for Maruja and stops being lightning coy. Now the sheer weight of the guitar calls to mind a Spanish Godzilla trashing entire blocks with a single massive sweep of his tail. The music is exhausting and numbing, it has become everything *flamenco* is not meant to be – heavy and odious. But this is only a warm-up for Maruja, a build-up for her ornamental fingers to start picking fake pears and for Byron's microtonal shifts. Soon the *falseta* (an embellishing or punctuating run) gives way to a *paseo* (melodic playing and fills).

The audience hoots and screams for more. According to Tall María, intellectuals reject *flamenco* because the Franco government uses it to attract tourists. They see it as a cheap selling of Spain to people who understand nothing of its essence. Maybe so, but for years I have practised *zapateado* in the mirror, so I follow exactly what Maruja is doing. She does not smile or look at the audience. Her back is arched, and her black hair pulled back tight, as shiny as a mirror. The rose behind her ear falls to the ground.

This does not look like the same woman who breathed so heavily in the Prado. Maruja dragged me from Goya, to Utrillo to Velásquez, and in each room she would go directly for the bench or couch and sit there fanning herself with her museum floorplan. The squat ugly royal *meninas*, imprisoned in their ruffles and bouffant silk sleeves, struck Maruja as especially interesting. I don't know. I considered those court paintings a waste of time, but Maruja was struck by their family life, and what the *meninas* must have sounded like and how they probably misbehaved.

Manolo preferred the naked ladies, especially the *Maja desnuda*. I found it hard to believe that some swanky important duchess would just lie there naked while she was being painted. But Manolo said clothes would only make her ugly.

Maruja did not like the Goya paintings of young women turning into hags and of patriots being executed. They made her cry and she did not want us spending much time in the Goya wing.

That day in Madrid, she dragged me to a large department store called El Corte Ingles, and there, after a few passes through ladies' shoes, Maruja had the courage to take me to the men's department. She tried on a man's round-toed brown sturdy walking shoe. Her foot was not long but wide. The salesman did not think it at all odd that she was buying a man's shoe, and I was thankful for that.

Anyway these are the clodhoppers that she now uses to do her heel-and-toe-clicking *flamenco*. They're so big they look like clown shoes. 'No salesperson in France would have allowed me to get away with that,' she exulted when we bought her shoes. I think she will go back there and get another pair.

I know that if I don't kiss Tall María tonight, someone else will. And this fills my chest with despair and 'if onlys'. Her hand feels small and light on my shoulder.

If that is how Byron rants and raves over a pair of baggy pants, what would he do if he were losing the love of his life?

I wipe my lips on Tall María's wrist. She pretends not to notice, but she moves her hand up my neck to my hair. I am happy Tall María is at my side, breathing softly and quietly.

Before leaving Villagarcía de Arosa, I again invite her to visit me in Paris. But I invite all of them in turn, one by one, Sofia, Teresa, Short María as well.

CHAPTER FOURTEEN

José-Ramón

The following year, at the age of thirteen, I am back in Pamplona for the San Fermín festival. My brother and I are sleeping on a bench. We have missed the last bus back to Maruja's house, and we don't have the courage to wake up Señora Gonzalez and ask to use her couch.

'Hey, hey . . . you Americano? Gotta match?'

It is 4 am, we are freezing and tired, and we have been trying to shut out the caterwauling of a bunch of drunken Italians and Dutch backpackers who are singing Toto Cotugno's macro-corny hit (copied by Fabian), '*Lassate mi cantaaaaaaaare*'.

'Hey, Americano, wake up!' A blond blue-eyed Basque, weaving on his heels, motions to his unlit cigarette. He stutters, grunts, repeats himself.

'You know Geminway, huh? Geminway was so drunk, he made a pass at my old lady. He did, I swear it.'

The blond, who has the neck of a bull, carries a bass drum which he keeps banging to punctuate his grunts.

'If he touched her with his magic wand, and she claims

he did, then I am Geminway junior. Look at me, open your eyes, you drunken shit! Gotta match?'

That is how we meet, through Hemingway's legendary sexual prowess: if you tell a Pamplonica you are American in Pamplona, his knee-jerk reaction will be to ask, '*Geminway?*' Few if any have ever read Hemingway, but there are countless photos of him in the *tabernas*. Over the cash registers you see him pictured at the bullring, wearing those fifties-style sunglasses. Every nostalgic or pretentious wannabe has a picture of Hemingway on his wall, it's about as unique as a glass of cheap wine. I often see his photo hung in the company of other Americans who have danced here during San Fermín, such as John Huston, Truman Capote, Ava Gardner. It's as if all these pictures had been taken in the exact same spot, in a front row seat at the bullring, behind the cushioned red leather of the first *barrera*.

For all my distrust of hype, there is a sense that Hemingway and his band of rich American hangers-on, adventurers, facilitators, millionaires, also-rans, struggling geniuses are somehow just touching my elbow, passing me like ghosts. We are passengers in the same train station, our paths crossing, each generation going its own way. The American divas and artists who came here to drink and play in the fifties aren't gone for good, they have only gone for a walk, leaving behind their photographs turning yellow on the wall.

José-Ramón Mina is nineteen and drives a produce truck

on the highways between Pamplona, Bilbao and Santander. He has never seen me before, but with his last hundred *pesetas* he buys me a drink, then buys me breakfast. So begins a special journey.

After the running of the bulls, José-Ramón invites me back to his home. For the rest of the week-long San Fermín fiesta I live in his house, and we become inseparable.

Maruja meets us by the bullring. She is worried about me and has brought me a change of socks, underwear and a sweater. But most importantly she wants to check the sort of boys I have fallen in with. She takes an immediate liking to José-Ramón: he is sober. His hair is combed, he smells good, and he is exceedingly polite to her.

'Nothing will happen to the *niño*, I swear, Señora Gonzalez.' (It is the only time I hear Maruja called that except by the *arrondissement* mayor who married her off.)

'He is my son,' says Maruja.

'Yes, I understand. I'll protect him like my own brother.'

His stuttering and trying to act formal only further endears him to Maruja. They talk about me as if I were some sort of delicate toy, I keep quiet about the running with the bulls.

'No harm will come to even a single hair on the boy's head,' says José-Ramón, resting his hand on his heart.

'I have to answer for him,' says Maruja, smiling at the oversized bull head. 'He is more my son than if I actually had a son. *Comprendes?* If anything goes wrong, I am responsible to his parents. He is only thirteen.'

'Señora Gonzalez, I won't let him run with the bulls, don't worry. And if the little bastard escapes my grip and tries to run, I will rip him to shreds.'

Maruja laughs, kisses me. She tells me to be careful, makes me promise not to come home late. She makes me put on a sweater which, after she leaves, I remove and tie around my waist, and lose in some bar that night.

After dancing in the street all night, every morning the same scenario is repeated: at 8 am José-Ramón's mother opens her front door, raises her hand to her mouth and with little cries of '*Por Dios, por Dios, por Dios*' bids us enter. She offers us soap, fresh towels and breakfast which we refuse, and closes the wooden shutters. Señora Mina is a little bit of a woman, Maruja's height, but thin and wispy. It is hard to imagine how she gave birth to such a giant. He towers above her, and when he bends to plant a kiss on her cheek she screams, 'Get away, you stink of booze and cigarettes, your father, God bless his soul, never allowed a drop of alcohol in this house.'

A single foam mattress is thrown on the floor for me. José-Ramón rips off his shirt and falls diagonally across his narrow bed, one arm above his head, and starts snoring within seconds of touching the pillow. His blond hair is sweating.

I hear Señora Mina tiptoe in to collect our dirty clothes

and go out without a word. I fall asleep smelling her son's strong armpit smells.

By 8.30 am every Pamplonico worth anything is sleeping.

At 3.30 pm Señora Mina wakes us up. José-Ramón, still in his wine-stained undershirt, tugs the sheets up over his head. My head feels better, but not much. The throbbing has stopped, but as I wobble unsteadily on my feet and go to urinate, I feel shaky. My body sags, heavy like one of those sodden stiff-leather wine gourds everyone carries here.

Señora Mina is on the phone with Maruja, explaining what she has prepared us for lunch, and how I am doing. I overhear Maruja's laughter cackling in the receiver.

I take a shower. It is one of those hand-held showerheads that looks like a telephone. There is no curtain around the tub, and I wash kneeling down, trying not to spray water all over the floor. My movements are jerky and tentative. I am still half asleep. It would take a month to dry out the cheap wine in my body. After another night of drinking and dancing through the streets, I move in slow motion through the fog.

My mouth is as dry as if it had been stuffed with cotton wool all night, my gums are hard and sore. Brushing my teeth, all I seem to find is bad breath – like those old men who have no teeth left to brush but do so out of nostalgia.

In Señora Mina's small kitchen, the sun is harsh and slanting through the window.

'How do you feel?' she smiles.

I nod, shading my eyes.

'Would you like some coffee?'

'*Sí, gracias.*' I never drink coffee, but I soon learn that during San Fermín this is the most important drink of the day, a black flushing that clears out the system. José-Ramón is buffaloing in his bathtub, making awful rutting and eructation sounds.

'You know,' whispers his mother, 'José drives his truck sometimes thirty hours straight, I tell him not to, because I get scared he will have an accident, but then he comes and sleeps here for two days straight, so I am used to this.'

'He has a heart of gold.'

'Yes, everyone likes him. His father was an engineer, but José never studied, he can't stand office life.'

There are pictures of Señor Mina up on the wall, but judging from the yellow sheen of the photos and the touched-up quality of his face, he has been long dead.

Each day Señora Mina prepares a potato and onion omelette, about two inches thick. When she slips it out of the frying pan on to the serving dish, I expect her to cut it in half, but instead she pushes it towards me, with a knife and fork on the side, a glass of seltzer water and a plastic basket full of sliced bread. I suggest she give half to José.

'No, no, he will get one of his own. Force yourself, your appetite will come. You need something in your system.'

Señora Mina's Spanish omelette covers the entire plate,

hanging over on the sides. I cut a piece and blow on it. The steam curls up into my blocked sinuses. I chew it with teeth that are still impacted in cotton wool. I eat mechanically, aware that my body functions, taste and smell are lurking somewhere deep inside. Eating helps me regenerate. Slowly I wake up.

José-Ramón enters the kitchen, holding on to the walls. His just-washed hair curls down his forehead into a V point between his eyebrows. He blinks and stutters. His new spotless white T-shirt clings to his body with moisture. His voice, gravelly from too much smoking and drinking and yelling at the bullfight, has been reduced to a hoarse whisper.

This meal is our breakfast, lunch and dinner all rolled into one. Neither José-Ramón nor I speak much, it takes too much effort, and it is not evident what we could possibly say. The silence in this small apartment is an oasis of sanity amid the fiesta chaos, as if Señora Mina were living not in Pamplona, but on some far planet.

She never complains, never suggests that we drink too much. A lifetime of San Fermíns has taken its toll on her. She fills our coffee cups without asking us and picks out our tickets for the afternoon's bullfight. She also lays our clothes out on the bed. All these simple tasks take on a huge significance in this week-long hangover.

On the bus José-Ramón and I stand semi-asleep, holding our spicy *chorizo* sandwiches wrapped in white paper. It is 5.30 pm.

On our way to the headquarters of Oberena, the *peña* or *jai alai* social club José-Ramón belongs to, we pass upper-class boys wearing crocodile shirts, shiny leather loafers, plaid pants and driving just-washed cars. Their women, covered in make-up and wearing high heels, ignore us as if we were street beggars.

Once inside Oberena's clubhouse, we down a glass of Martini Rosso. José-Ramón is one of two bass drummers in the marching band. It is a role which suits his strength and personality – any guff from police, or from uptight bourgeois, or competing clubs gets drowned out in a roll of thuds.

I adjust the leather straps on the back of his shoulders. He never complains of the weight or the strain, but as soon as he dons this massive drum his whole body tilts backwards like a woman about to give birth. At the bar we quaff another two glasses of wine. It is never clear to me who pays when we are out in taverns, but in the clubhouse, drinks are free to the band members, and as José's underage sidekick I am included in the largesse. The bartenders also fill our leather wine gourds for free.

The rest of the band comes limping in; some are still getting dressed and rubbing sleep from their eyes. They gulp down coffees, light a first cigarette, grab their instruments. There is some back slapping. But unlike the evenings, they don't even ask for a drink, they just stand at the bar, faces white, hands shaky, and wait to be served like young businessmen waiting for a commuter train.

Where were you last night, José? Did they arrest you? They should have arrested you! Did the waterhoses get you this morning? I looked for you at 7 am on Calle de la Estafeta. Where did you start your run?

Now we are ready. The band assembles, and we push out into the sunlight. José-Ramón starts pounding on his drum. The staccato explosions and the wine bring him slowly back to life.

The day is already hot and the streets are divided into black shade and dazzling white sunlight. One does not just enter the bullring, one makes an entrance. Our *peña* theme song is one of the ageless anthems of the fiesta:

> *¡O-be-rena!*
> *es la peña de más alegría*
> *¡O-be-rena!*
> *La que no tiene rival.*
>
> *Pamplona seis de Julio*
> *bullicio y alegría*
> *ya están los Pamplonicos*
> *ansiosos de gozar.*
> *Con faja, pañuelico,*
> *la bota de clarete*
> *con el primer cohete,*
> *la juerga va a empezar.*

The band could play this in their sleep; the lyrics are so ingrained one hears mothers singing it to their babies. The first three drumbeats, each separate, underline the name of the *peña*: *O*, then *be*, then *rena* – 'the best' in Basque – and this repeated triumvirate has the simplicity of a call to arms: if you hear it, and it is July, and you are in the Basque capital, your shoulders and legs start dancing of their own accord.

It is not far to the bullring. Behind the band, latecomers are hurrying in.

Oberena is the oldest and best endowed of the *peñas*, and it flaunts a *noblesse oblige* attitude towards the other clubs vying to win soccer matches and intramural *jai alai* competitions. They're sort of like the New York Yankees – having won so many tournaments in the past, they now assume a lofty indifference to the fact that other clubs regularly beat them.

In the square outside the ring, we wait for more stragglers. It is important for the ethos of the *peña* to have as many Oberenans making as much hoo-haa as possible when we enter the ring. Police and ticket collectors cast a weary eye in our direction. We are careful to ignore the riff-raff of other *peñas* collecting on the square. No one wants fisticuffs this early in the day.

Gypsies are selling carnations and sprigs of rosemary for good luck (also as cures for premature baldness, impotence, frigidity, bad luck in love, family disharmony, money problems and drought).

Carriages with brilliant livery disgorge their wealthy occupants, men with macassared hair and tie-pins; women in traditional dresses or smart suits, like theatre-goers at an opening night. They say the mother of the pretender to the throne, the Duchess of Alba and other titled grandees are attending this year.

We ignore the ill-smelling unshaved foreigners, many German and Swedish backpackers who have no clue about proper San Fermín tauromachy etiquette, or the importance of the morning siesta. Foreigners have been drinking all morning, they stink of barf and cheap wine, and they stumble towards the bullring with matted hair and dirty haggard faces. We let them pass as if they were a colony of lepers. They don't know you are supposed to dress up for a *corrida* out of respect for the bull.

Tourists go to a bullfight out of curiosity, they don't have the poison (as *aficionados* call it). Some even argue with the ticket sellers whether they can just go in for the twenty-five minutes it takes to dispatch one bull, rather than have to sit through all six bulls.

Foreign women (especially the blondes) attract greedy attention during San Fermín nights, but in the light of day these sirens look as unkempt and bedraggled as their disreputable men. And the Pamplonicas who swore undying love and admiration to them last night ignore them today. The fallen angels sit on the kerb, rubbing their dirty sandalled feet, talking foreign gibberish and asking in a gruff voice where the nearest pharmacy is.

For our entrance into the ring, no one is wine-stained yet, not one member of the *peña* is sweating yet. Our white shirts and white pants, creases pressed to perfection, shine in the sun. There are national TV cameras here and a horde of journalists. In view of all that will take place later, it is important that we arrive looking like choirboys. So the band is well-combed, clean-shaven, exuding innocence and youth. Soon José-Ramón will be sweating like a horse, but for now he still smells semi-sweet, his breath fresh, and his underarms retain a trace of body soap. He has the muscles of a horse, his back and arms are as hard as rock.

CHAPTER FIFTEEN

Sol y sangre

At 5.15 pm we take our reserved seats. Bullfights are the
only events that start on time in Spain, and for the *peñas*
they always start three-quarters of an hour early. We're in
the middle of the *Sol* section, high up in the stands – the
equivalent of baseball bleachers. Here the sun is smack in
our eyes; the heat is so intense, and the enormous quantities
of wine meant to keep us from dehydration only make us
hotter and thirstier.

This year El Cordobés appears for the first time at the
San Fermín festival. And unfortunately for him, he has a
John-Paul-Ringo fringe of long hair which he keeps flicking
out of his eyes. Bullfighters often grow their hair long in the
back and twist it into a small brilliantined ponytail, perhaps
an atavistic bow to the bull's tail, or to the gypsy origins of
the *vaqueros*. But the fringe which El Cordobés flicks just-
washed out of his eyes is anathema to the crowd's *machos*.

El Cordobés is the best-known young bullfighter in
Spain. Thanks in part to his good looks, and his habit of
facing the bull with the cape down on the sand or behind

him, he has become a media darling. That is another reason we hate him. His publicity, his foreign TV interviews, his autobiography, cast him as bullfighter of the century. But no one here trusts the new or the gimmicky. Fans remember Dominguín (Hemingway's buddy and Ava Gardner's husband), and they still revere Manolete, the dour-faced Babe Ruth of bullfighting who was gored to death on Aug. 28, 1947, Juan Belmonte who grew up a street urchin in Seville, even Paul Romero, the eighteenth-century Seville legend. These heroes are lay saints, their pictures glued on kitchen walls, above stoves and *taberna* sinks and restaurant bars, and no amount of TV hype will give their mantle or heritage to El Cordobés without him earning it fair and square.

'*Corta'tel pelo, corta'tel pelo!*' (Cut your hair), the *peñas* keep chanting, and '*Eres muy malo, eres muy malo!*' (You're very bad.)

When he tries his patented groin-first advance towards the bull, dragging the cape behind him and inching right up to the horns – an act which from any other bullfighter would bring an ovation of love and respect – the sun-drenched boys boo El Cordobés for being too showy, a *chulo*, an egomaniacal publicity hound, a male impersonator. He could strangle the bull with his bare hands, and no one in *Sol* would respect him. Anyway it's the bravery of the bull, not the bullfighter, that is paramount.

Every bullring has its share of crackpots who, fortified by abundant sherry, shout advice to the *matador* and draw laughter from the crowd. But the bleachers in Pamplona are especially infamous for the intensity of their adulation and scorn. The president of Oberena's youth league leaps up and roars into a paper megaphone, 'You less-than-man weakling wimp queer ass-licking troubadour lesbian facilitator adventurist, invalid moronic hoo-haa cut your hair!'

And our refrain, many-times repeated, is, '*Corta'tel pelo, eres muy malo!*'

Of course, it is absurd to accuse the son of a poor farmworker who is risking his life in front of a seven-hundred-kilo Miura bull of wanton cowardice, but our drunkenness knows no logic. The vision of a bullfighter – the epitome of all that is manly in Spain – having womanly hair touches a raw nerve.

'Cut your hair, or we'll bury you!'

And on this particularly hot day when José-Ramón pours wine into my shoes ('There, now you are like Christ the fisherman,' he explains), we do bury El Cordobés. Someone has smuggled in his effigy in a wooden casket draped in black, and they parade it around with loud lamentations and set it on fire.

'Cut your hair, you fop, you unsurpassed phoney mother-offending deballed cuckold castrated cross-dresser!'

I am shouting with the rest of them, but I almost feel sorry for El Cordobés. His hair is longish, about Beatle length in the front, but quite short in the back.

He earns an ear. The judges are trying to be fair, trying not to be influenced by the mob. No doubt they want to reward such a national figure for deigning to grace the *feria* with his presence and his attendant publicity – but when he takes a lap of honour around the ring, supposedly to collect flowers and ovations, we start tossing him our *chorizo* sandwiches, our seat cushions, our empty bottles, and of course our large plastic saw-tooth combs. It is raining wolf whistles and junk on the ring. Soon the sand is littered, and El Cordobés double-times it back to the protective cover of his assistants' capes. He runs to avoid the charred casket that hurtles towards him. His running away only confirms what we have always known.

'You were born unsexed, you wear horns, you hermaphrodite, you belong in a satrap of eunuchs and ladies-in-waiting!'

El Cordobés never returns to fight in Pamplona.

I head for the toilets. My rope-soled San Fermín sandals are squishy and squeak with the wine José-Ramón poured into them. The toilet is so full of men, I head for the facilities located in the more expensive shaded section.

After my pee, I take a peek at the *Sombra* section just as a flair of trumpets is introducing the next *matador*. (There are three basic price ranges for seats: *Sol*, facing direct sunlight for the whole of the fight, are cheapest; *Sol y Sombra*, which get shade half-way through, come next; and *Sombra*, shaded throughout, are the most expensive.)

It's another world here in *Sombra*. Here sit the patricians robed in grave dignity, city and provincial officials, the judges who award ears and tails, middle-aged *majas* (untouchable beauties dressed in nineteenth-century lace shawls and ornate combs). From here the bullfight proceeds with choreographed exactitude, the uniformed band playing *pasodobles* and *jotas*. It reminds me of the bullfight that Uncle Joaquín took me to see in Madrid. Even though I was glad to be with my favourite uncle and two pretty cousins, it was a morose, lifeless affair, like having a professor describe a symphony as air being pushed through a collection of musical instruments. They could be watching TV! There is no hoopla, no madness.

El Viti dedicates his next bull to the judges first, then the *majas*, and finally the entire ring.

Across the way in blazing white sunlight I see banners, stands full of yobbos and yahoos chanting. The Roman plebs, at its most pitiless and unruly. Few bullfighters take the risk of removing their hat and dropping it at the feet of the *Sol* section, because hounds from hell couldn't flatter this rabble.

The *Sombra* audience casts such a dispassionate look on life and death, I am happy for the *Guardia Civil* who asks for my ticket and waves me back towards the wolves.

Carried by tumultuous cries of *olé* (according to Joaquín, a corruption of Allah), I return towards the cheapo seats which century-old tradition reserves for each of the dozen *peñas*.

El Viti is the opposite of El Cordobés – a steady veteran who will never rise to the status of genius, but he does all the *verónicas* (wiping the cape over the bull's face as the saint did to Christ), all the backward passes and inward trills with economy and restraint and good workmanlike style. He never takes a cheap shot, never tries to wow the crowd, and today we give him more *olés* than he deserves, we pay homage to his conservatism, knowing El Cordobés is watching.

Roasting in the sun, José-Ramón squirts wine into my mouth, and he does it from such a distance that the jet splashes my face and neck. I beg him to stop. There is a way of drinking from a gourd, just opening your throat, which every Pamplonico knows but which I never master. Every time I swallow wine slams into my teeth. By now our gourd wine is hot from the baking sun. José-Ramón crawls over to the *peña* cooler and grabs an ice-cold bottle of Martini Rosso. This we pass around almost religiously, not wasting a single drop. As the afternoon draws on, José-Ramón steals ice from the cooler, rubs it on his forehead, and when I least suspect it slips a cube down my shirt. It's such a hot and sweaty day, I don't mind this, or more wine in my shoes.

Something is wrong with El Viti today. The *olés* have stopped. No one is booing yet, but neither are we impressed. He's not himself. He seems nervous, wimpish, muddle-headed, frightened of risk, incapable of controlling the rhythm of the bull. 'It's a bad bull,' says José-Ramón, 'it's not his fault. He's erratic, unpredictable.'

But great *matadors* must overcome bad bulls.

El Viti gives up and goes for the *muleta* or short scarlet cape used only at the end; he tries to put the bull to death quickly. The first time, he puts the sword over the bull's horns into the bull's neck, instead of sliding right into the heart; the sword slams into the shoulder bone and the bull trots away. This is what I don't like. We start booing. The second sword thrust goes in up to the hilt, but evidently it misses because the bull is still standing. El Viti has to pull the sword out. He knows he deserves the heckling he gets. On the third try, which really ought to be the *coup de grâce*, the bull charges at the last second and the sword goes behind the shoulder blade. Now we are up, whistling and jeering. El Viti's assistants come out and try to get the bull to fall down on the sand by dizzying him with their capes. El Viti waves them away. The bull stands there, his head down, waiting to be put out of his suffering.

This is real shitty.

It reminds me of the time Maruja and I saw a *novillero* (young bullfighter) who plunged his sword into the bull a dozen times, twice missing the shoulders completely and sticking him in the upper thigh, before the animal fell to the sand. Maruja tried to cover my eyes, but I swore to myself that my father was right, that there was no justification for such inhumanity.

El Viti's fourth plunge is almost perfect. The bull backs up against the restraining barrier, coughing up blood, but still refuses to fall to the sand. Poor El Viti is having a bad day, but the animal is standing there vomiting blood, and as always I wish the bull and the bullfighter had their roles reversed, just for once.

I sit down. The men standing on their toes shade me, their steaming, wine-sodden bodies grant me a little haven of coolness. Anyway I prefer to follow the drama by listening to them roar.

In the *Sol* bleachers, we miss entire bulls. It's like sitting through the second game of a double-header that goes into extra innings. No one cares if a double *verónica* is followed by a twirl-away. Whenever I see a handsome fresh bull charge, and I see the *picador* leaning in on his lance to dig in a large red gash as deep as a well, which leaves the proud animal not yet dying, but his muscles and innards hanging out of him, I unconsciously remember the movie I saw with Tall María and Manolo.

It was a maudlin low-budget black-and-white film in which a seven-year-old boy who sees his beloved bull enter a ring dashes out into a ministry building down endless corridors trying to find someone who will save the bull's life. The scenes intercut dramatically, with shots of the bull being caped and leaping over the restraining walls. Of course bullfights occur on religious feast days (from April to November) when anyone with an office job is at the ring, but in the movie the good Falangist governor and all his assistant paper-pushers are hard at work in their offices, and the boy talks his way past countless guards and major-domos, and just in time convinces the governor to save the bull. I cried like a baby. So did Tall María.

I can't explain why, but as much as I love sitting here

with José-Ramón, I am also suspending disbelief and running down that hallway praying for some bureaucrat to spare the bull's life. This is sentimental and false. Without bullfighting there would be no such bulls (*toros bravos*), for these are bred solely to die in the *corrida*.

Maruja once took me to a Portuguese bullfight just south of the Galician border, in which the bullfighter was on horseback and the bull's life was spared. She asked me afterwards if I liked it.

'Yes,' I said. The aesthetics of horse and rider, and coloured ribbons were nice. But it left me cold and uninvolved.

Was it the lack of death that I missed? Was it José-Ramón and the besotted *peñas* from hell that I missed?

My father says, 'Bullfighting is a cruel bloodsport for the uncivilized,' and I suppose he is objectively right, but to watch a bullfight dispassionately and coolly is to miss its real meaning. I never manage to explain this to him, or to myself. What most offends my father's notions of fair play is the fact that the outcome for the bull is known before the fight begins and therefore it cannot be called a 'sport'. The Spanish newspapers don't run it in their sports pages, but in the Arts and Leisure section, under *Espectáculo*. Maybe it is a kind of vice, like sex or drugs. Maybe, as Geminway said, it is simply a 'tragedy'.

After El Viti, little swarthy Paco Camino steps in. He walks to the centre of the ring and gets down on his knees.

This is his trademark. There is a hush. The first rush of a fresh bull is the deadliest and everyone in the crowd knows this. When the bull charges out and heads straight for Paco Camino, he takes his cape and twirls it above his head as the bull goes by.

That is all he needs to do for us – ever.

The *picador* is fat and old and I keep praying he will be upended. When he is and has to scoot for safety, the poor blindfolded horse thrown on its side struggling to stand under all its padding, we cheer wildly.

Paco puts in his own *banderilla*. And while the *olés* from the *Sol* section are harder to come by at first than those of *Sombra*, ours mean more and, once we get going, we overwhelm the ring. We want a hero today, and we are drunker than usual because Señora Mina's sandwich, which sops up some of the wine, was tossed at El Cordobés and swept up by the clean-up crew.

When Paco is awarded both ears and the tail of the last bull of the day, his supporters rush out to carry him in triumph around the ring. The fancy beshawled ladies and the bourgeois in the shade sections head for home, but for us the real fiesta begins. We tumble down the tiers towards the safety barriers, jump over and unfurl our banners.

We gather in the ring. Each *peña* is preceded by a long white flag painted by a cartoonist. During the street dancing, this banner ought never to droop, but should bounce along as madly as possible. Carrying one of the poles is a huge honour, and because I am under-age and there is

179

always a risk some zealous *Guardia Civil* will kick me out of the parade, I always volunteer to carry the banner.

Holding the pole with both hands, I kick my knees up and twirl around. This is tiring. The pole is about three metres high and the wind and the crowd pull you off balance. It's like dancing with a demanding mistress – you keep going until you drop or someone taps you on the shoulder and cuts in.

As we head out of the ring, I hear a familiar scream. It is Maruja waving and calling me over. She kisses and hugs me and screams with horror at the wine on my shirt and pants. She laughs at the dirt on my sandals and in my hair, the buttons ripped off José-Ramón's shirt, the ashes of El Cordobés' casket on his hands. Then she howls, '*Niño, niño!* What a terrible blister on your heel! Come on, give up that banner and show me your heel. Don't argue!'

Madmen are dancing by, banging each other on the head with rubber hammers, screaming, and Maruja has my heel on her lap, and she is squeezing out pus, pushing the end of a safety pin into the skin. José-Ramón beating on his drum drowns out my howls of pain. When the wound is clean, Maruja puts on a band-aid and screams for me to be careful.

Soon we are swept away by the *peña*.

Once out of the ring, we dance through streets packed on both sides with spectators. I feel unemployed without the banner to carry. A girl dances by, and I pinch her breast. She turns and slaps my face. José-Ramón grabs her. 'Why did you do that?'

'He knows why!' She pushes her chin out at me.

José stares in mute incomprehension. 'What did you do, *niño*?'

'A tit went by and I grabbed it.'

José-Ramón presents all his excuses to the girl and we dance on. 'What is the matter with you, *hombre*?'

'I did the first thing that went through my head.'

'This isn't America, here we act nobly.'

Maybe it's the wine, maybe it's my dream of visiting Tall María and kissing her right under Uncle Joaquín's nose that has beclouded my mind.

All the *peñas* follow a pre-set parade course from the bullring through the streets, and people watch from balconies and stands. But today, Oberena carries Paco Camino to his five-star hotel where the TV cameras are waiting. His gold-trimmed tight-fitting silk costume, a *traje de luces* (suit of lights) which costs about five thousand dollars, is sweat-soaked and he must be freezing in the evening cold, though he keeps waving and casting a brave smile at his adoring public.

Back at our clubhouse José-Ramón drops off his bass drum. The leather shoulder straps have cut deep grooves into his skin and I massage his aching lower back. Even without the drum, he's so sore he still waddles like a pregnant woman.

It is time now for a belated dinner.

Where does the evening go? What do we do? I follow José-Ramón. The bacchanalia continues all night. I kill fifty thousand brain cells, easy, and no doubt this is a conservative estimate. There are revellers vomiting in the gutter, and others sleeping on benches. There are men quarrelling, pouring wine at each other, snapping their fingers with their arms up in the air. But by American standards the drunks here are good-natured, the potential for violence is subdued, mostly exchanges of words drowned out in hoarse singing.

José-Ramón and I end up cut off from the rest of the *peña*, in the fairgrounds on the outskirts of town. We are too drunk to drive bumper cars or test our strength on the hammer throw. We have no money left, and I am tired.

We enter a large striped canvas tent and find ourselves facing a brightly lit elevated stage. The tent is full of sweaty inebriated men, smoking and kicking up dust from the dirt floor, shouting crude epithets at the empty stage. Distorted stripper music blares from speakers under the stage, and suddenly women wearing only feathers, fishnet stockings and halter tops prance out from both wings of the stage. They have tassels on their breasts. For Franco's Spain this is incredibly racy and risqué. I am not certain how at thirteen I have managed to sneak in here; even at nineteen I doubt José-Ramón is allowed here, and neither of us has paid.

I have never seen such big fat thighs. From my vantage point these women look like Percheron horses, but José-

Ramón doesn't seem to mind, he starts whistling and hollering like all the other men. They start clapping in unison. These Percheron ladies are grotesque, belong in a freak show, but the men, blind and mad with alcohol, don't see what I see.

'What gams, what gams, kiss me darling, blow us a kiss!' howls José-Ramón, clapping to the music. I've never seen him show any interest in women, but he too is frothing at the mouth like some depraved seasick sailor.

The Clydesdale women are not doing anything sexy, they're just marching in place, in their tinsel red boots, but that is enough for the men. I feel embarrassed for José-Ramón whistling and hooting, sorry for all these slobs, their shirts torn and sweaty, pants encrusted with mud, sorry also for the Percherons, who keep smiling and walking in place like idiots.

I think of Tall María and her skinny legs. If I had her here I would let her take me to a secluded spot in a pine forest where I would kneel and lick the poison from her wounded foot; I would do this even if she were not wounded.

It is 2 am. I tell José-Ramón I am hungry. He never cares about eating, but finding me food is something he takes seriously. We walk back into town searching for a restaurant that might extend us credit. I am happy to have José-Ramón back all to myself. Had a Percheron winked at him I would be alone now. It shocks me how evanescent friendship can be between men.

For dinner, José-Ramón swears me to secrecy. He ties his sweaty red neckerchief tight around my eyes, then turns me around and leads me blind down the street. Peeking under the blindfold, I follow him up three flights. When he unbandages my eyes, he clamps his hands on my mouth and indicates for me to shut up. This is the kick-in-the-pants school of conversation. José-Ramón points for me to look around, but repeatedly brings his index fingers to his lips. A profoundly unwordy man, when he gets drunk he prefers to mime his meaning.

We are in an illegal school which teaches children Basque, a language outlawed by Franco. José-Ramón shows me drawings of tortures inflicted on Basque freedom fighters – Franco policies explained in drawings for children. I see limbs in jars of formaldehyde, fingers, ears, penises, even a leg that looks like a wax reproduction, but José-Ramón assures me it is real.

He heats up some soup and makes us sandwiches – the politics of the belly. They know him here, but it's not clear how involved he is with them. For the rest of the night, and on through our running with the bulls, whenever I mention the Basque hideout or ETA terrorists, he brings his index finger to his lips and motions that he will cut my head off.

CHAPTER SIXTEEN

Teresa: the smile of the buddha

Maruja and Manolo have finally adopted a round-cheeked baby girl who looks as fat and happy as Maruja. They call her María Cariño. Maruja dotes on her, drowns her in as much love as she heaped on me.

When I meet the two-year-old baby and see Maruja kissing her and hugging her, I feel odd, embarrassed in a way.

'Isn't she beautiful, beautiful?' Maruja keeps gushing.

I nod and mumble yes, but Cariño does not look pretty at all, she looks rather plain to me, a fat little piglet sleeping in her pram. Maruja can't stop kissing this interloper. She hugs me too. 'Don't worry, you'll always be my baby.' But at thirteen I don't need to be babied, and yet suddenly I find myself running to my room crying. I lie in bed counting the seconds Maruja will take to leave her overweight baby and come to my room and hug me. It's too long, too long. It seems totally unfair that a baby who has done nothing, said nothing, should suddenly get so much attention. Eventually Maruja lumbers down the hallway. I hear her say, 'Where is my big baby, my big silly boy?' She sits down on the bed and the mattress sags half-way down to the floor. She kisses me. I shove my face into my pillow and hide. I don't need her pity, and I don't want her to think she can buy me off so easily. She wraps me in her arms and holds me. Her kitchen fried and soapy dish smells are more distant, more impersonal to me.

'There, there, *niño*.'

Blessedly, I don't see much of Cariño because after fifteen years in Paris, Maruja and Manolo have saved up enough to retire and live middle-class lives in dirt-poor Galicia.

When they leave our service, Maruja and Manolo stand in the living-room in their Sunday best and she can't stop crying and asking me if I am upset. I tell her I am not at all upset – it's nothing I can control, but clearly it seems to me all this is her fault, all due to adopting Cariño.

They return to work in Paris during the winter, sometimes working for us, but they spend the rest of the time on the beach, renting out the top two floors of their house to German families. They continue to invite me to stay with them.

One of my many hopeless invitations for my cousins to join me – letters written out of despair with no expectation of success – is, to my eternal surprise, answered in the affirmative. The following year Teresa joins me for San Fermín. Her mother lets her come because Maruja is there to chaperone us. But Maruja is now completely obsessed with Cariño, and knowing this gives Teresa and me the luxury of spending time alone.

Teresa is shy, she wears a blue denim shirt, denim pants. She has a sweet smile, with thick black curls down past her neck. It is odd to be fourteen and walking around in Pamplona, free and on my own with Teresa. For two hours or so I don't dare touch her or hold her hand. I have never done this kind of thing in broad daylight before. Finally, terrified, fearful that some society matron or secret agent of my aunt, or Teresa herself, will scream, I venture to hold her fingers. She does not push me away, but maintains her quiet timid half-smile.

This is the first time I have held hands in the street with a girl (no need for the protective darkness of a movie theatre). The first morning together we are soon walking arm-in-arm, but hardly speaking.

It's the day before San Fermín begins, and we hang out down by the bull corrals outside the city walls with a bunch of gypsy boys. I try to get rid of them, but they follow us. I want to be alone with Teresa, want to be away in some hotel room, but we are staying with Maruja, and she would never allow that.

We spend the rest of the afternoon on a bench, interlaced like a couple of squid. I have my hand under her blue-jean shirt on the flat of her back. There seems to be no limit to what she will let me do, and this frightens me. Teresa falls asleep with her head on my shoulder. I smell her hair and become acquainted with every follicle. I kiss her little ears. But I don't have the guts to go further, anyway I wouldn't know what to do, or where or with what. Especially not with Uncle Alfonso a mere ten hours away by train.

Why is it I remember these hours of Teresa in my arms, our puppy love, better than many mature relations I have had since? The power of memory magnifies and deepens, but I am not certain that in this case the re-creation is a falsification. I truly loved Teresa.

As she dozes, I watch over her, with one hand around her waist, the other feeling the elastic of her bra. Teresa will have a child out of wedlock, she will shock her family and go off and be an artist in Holland, but for now she and I don't know where to go, or how to proceed. We have come as far as we can.

Early evening, I take her to Araceli's bakery. Some things never change. Araceli is still there, standing in the exact same spot on the left as you enter, behind the glass display case of pastries. The cashier seated at the back and the old crone at the ovens are there too, but the bakery is just as gloomy as I remember it. Smaller and dingier perhaps. I get Araceli's permission for Teresa and me to sleep on the couch if we miss the last bus back to Maruja's. (Are my designs not transparent? Can Araceli be so naïve?)

'No, no, come any time, my darlings,' she keeps saying. 'Go there right now! Mama will give you your own key.'

Señora Gonzalez gives us a key so we can come and go as we please. She calls Maruja, and they agree it is a good idea for us to stay in the centre of town, rather than having to commute back and forth to the outskirts. In the stone-cold staircase of the Gonzalez apartment building, Teresa and I kiss. It is our first real kiss on the lips, and her breath is as sweet as dandelion floss. If the tiles were not so cold and if we knew how, we would make love right here on the stairs, or perhaps standing in a darkened doorway. For now our hips join, our bodies hug, we love each other desperately through our blue jeans until our lips grow raw.

Teresa and I rush out to see the fireworks. These are not New York City July Fourth rockets that rise from some unreachable waterfront at the horizon, fireworks that you watch from miles away, barely lifting your head. In Pamplona, the fireworks are fired in the central square, a few metres from where we stand, and Teresa and I watch from the bandstand as men rush around lighting all the rockets.

'*Oh, mira el rojo! Mira el azul!*' I squeeze her.

'*Mira, mira, mira!*'

We both crane our necks back ninety degrees. For years I came here and watched these with Maruja, my head resting on her ample bosom, and she held me from behind to prevent me from falling over. Tonight I hold Teresa from behind, and it is delicious because everyone's eyes are turned to the sky. Giant jonquils envelop us in their downward-racing petals. We scream and duck, expecting the red and green lights to enter our pupils and burn our eyelids. The sky is thick with gunpowder. When a rocket misfires, the crowd screams, but not even the *Guardia Civil* advises us to move back.

'*Aie   aie   aie,   los   amarillos,   oooooooo   mira. AAAAAIIIEE!*'

Spent fireworks cloud the sky. New flashes of yellow and red light up in a fog of grey. Bang, bang, bang. Silver sparkles fall earthward. Those that explode as soon as they clear the mortar tube render us deaf. To protect Teresa, I envelop her in my arms. The organizers wait for the wind to clear away the smoke. We don't move.

'*Oh, el verde! Aie que bonitos los amarillos!*'

For the last set of fireworks, ten different rockets go up at once. The sky is obliterated. Blues and reds fill up the night. After the last grand finale, I close my eyes and lose myself in Teresa's embrace. We wait for the crowd to disperse.

'There are too many drunks, let's go,' says Teresa.

I show her the fairgrounds, the old bumping cars I used to love. I stop at the shooting stand where Maruja and Manolo watched me so many times collect points. The guy has the same crummy airguns, the same wrought-iron stand with the white balls that you shoot off their little perch. He doesn't say a word to me, just stands there jingling coins in his blue apron. I'm looking at the varnished wooden wine casket with the three little copper goblets that has inflated from four hundred and fifty to five hundred and fifty points. I can't believe that is what I wasted so much of Maruja's money on, that absurd souvenir. A man plonks down a *duro* and picks up a carbine. I watch him fit in the little metal pellet. He doesn't aim at the balls, he shoots the white clay pipes.

To gain courage and resolve for what I want to do with Teresa, I drink one-*peseta* shots of wine and she waits patiently at my side. This is the cheapest rotgut in *tabernas*, a timeless cheapness that bespeaks of the vinegar fermenting in Ludivino's stable. A few moments later, I bend over and vomit on the side of the road. The wine is so tart and thick, that even as it comes up, it burns my throat and makes me sick all over again.

Teresa does not say a word, she holds me. Her black hair is frizzy on the sides at her temple, but semi-long in the back and held in a loose ponytail. She has a triangular chin that ends in a point like a cat, and little round chipmunk cheeks which I keep wanting to bite. Her eyes are dark but keep veering to green or grey, and even at night blue. She often gives me a mute smile, lips almost open, as if she were about to burst out laughing, but not quite.

We continue back into town. Purple-mouthed, I feel sober now, chastened and humbled, but I walk with my arm tightly around her, feeling she is a true ally.

Teresa walks half asleep, her eyes closing. Returning to where old Señora Gonzalez will be padding about, in those felt shoe coverings to protect her parquet floors, makes no sense. Though half deaf, she will hear every sound we make. I also steer clear of the Oberena clubhouse because I know if I see José-Ramón, he will take me away from

Teresa, and I do not want anything to ruin our time together. We return to our bench on the Plaza Mayor.

Here we're surrounded by drunken taurine critics and foreign revellers, but at least we don't have to worry about Manolo's mother and sister spying on us. We have no place to be private, no room, couch, cave, so this becomes a night of longing and desire.

We are dozing arm-in-arm, when street cleaners roust us with their water cannon. We take refuge on the bandstand from which we saw the fireworks display.

It is 4 am, Teresa and I are freezing, tired, and a band of drunken Spaniards approaches, looking for an argument, a cigarette, offering us their wine gourds. 'You *Americanos*?' Teresa and I take shelter in a *taberna*. A patron asks, 'Are you two *novios*? Fiancés?'

I blush. 'No, just cousins.'

'Cousins?'

I expect someone in the bar to ask me my age or comment that how I hold Teresa is not the way cousins ought to hold each other, but the sweaty drunken men don't seem to mind. She is so young and vulnerable amid these men, she whispers, 'Hold me tight, Alfonsito, don't leave me alone.'

I am her protection from the night. But what Teresa said to her folks to get their permission to come here alone is a mystery to me. What Maruja must be saying now when they call her from Vigo for news, all this baffles me.

★

To be avoiding José-Ramón and be sneaking around his city during his *feria* is bad enough, but to be doing so on account of a girl makes me feel doubly guilty. It's not simply a question of disloyalty, there is something mean and unholy about it.

I search for the Basque hideout that José-Ramón showed me. The answers I get are specious. With ETA separatists blowing up police stations and banks, everyone is scared to talk. Teresa and I stop kissing long enough to locate what I recall was the street and the building. The restaurant owner on the first floor denies any knowledge of what I am talking about, then he warns me to leave and not come back.

I don't know who tells me. Maybe I dream it. Maybe I knew it all along, that I would regret hiding from José-Ramón, that there was no reason to hide. Full of prepared lies and excuses, I call Señora Mina, but there is no answer. Is she out of town? What could have happened in a year? Did he die in some truck accident? Has José-Ramón married and settled down somewhere?

The Oberena clubhouse is full of older couples, and no one there remembers José-Ramón Mina. It's a large club, and José-Ramón was not a luminary. He just banged the hell out of their bass drum. Teresa and I are allowed in only because I mention Jesús, the president of their youth league.

Tonight Oberena is a sedate *jai alai* club, with women in high heels, and men in suits sharing pricey drinks.

'Have you seen José-Ramón Mina?' I keep asking the bartenders. They shrug. It's a busy night.

Jesús is surrounded by people asking him for favours, for keys, waiting on his orders. He is slick and polished, with a self-conscious charm and a perfectly combed parting on the side of his head. I never liked how José-Ramón fell silent around him, acting like a poor slob, pulling his forelock. Once Jesús asked me, 'So how's it living with a truck driver?' It was as if he was expecting me to make fun of José-Ramón. Around Jesús, you have to be witty and bright, a life enhancer, a raconteur, or you don't last long. José-Ramón with his illiterate stutter and his thumps on the drum never made the grade.

When I ask Jesús as to his whereabouts, he too pretends ignorance.

'My truck-driver friend, José, remember him? He was blond and handsome and poured wine in my shoes?'

I wish I had the guts to tell Jesús, José-Ramón is the best thing Spain has produced since Don Quixote. He had the heart of a saint, the muscle of a bull, and you, Jesús, with your high-society high-heeled women, your *jai alai* wall and your fancy bartenders, are a prissy pretentious asshole not to realize it. Eat shit and die. Jesús, you don't have an ounce of the balls that José-Ramón had.

Maybe he senses my mood, because he doesn't answer my shit-eating smile, but keeps walking right past me.

Women are not allowed to run with the bulls. And Teresa

gives me no argument when I accompany her back to Señora Gonzalez's apartment and put her to sleep on the couch.

I want to sleep too, but out of loyalty (or perhaps guilt), I go alone to the bar where José-Ramón and I used to repair at 6 am in preparation for the run. It feels weird here without him. I keep imagining I will die this morning, in this running. The presentiment is so strong I can't shake it. Out of loyalty to José-Ramón, I order a cognac and a sherry. With him I never once thought of danger. And whenever he spoke of his fears, I would laugh, call him a coward. But now I am scared, I feel sober again. I've betrayed my friend, and he is making me pay for my Faustian bargain.

I don't like cognac. I stand at the bar watching the sky lighten through the window.

Because it is fiesta time, the entire city is up at 6.15 am. In the bar a group of older men with jackets and ties stand talking. With them is probably a granddaughter. The girl keeps staring at me, and I at her. She is about Teresa's age, only taller, she reminds me of Tall María. I fall in love with her, just staring at her. She is facing me and the old men have their backs turned towards me and are busy talking so they don't see the love in my eyes. This is a nation full of Uncle Joaquíns and beautiful Teresas. The girl, arms crossed, holding a sweater, stares unabashedly, knowing the older men protect her.

I lean up against the bar, feeling alone and exceedingly

dramatic. I am waiting for the first *cohete* to announce the bulls that will kill me. Somehow having Teresa in my arms all day and night, at my mercy, has empowered me, made me bold, as if I have all the accoutrements of manhood. It's a game of mirrors. The fact they think I possess Teresa gives me confidence.

I tell the dark girl with my eyes that if I am gored this morning, my death is for her. If I live, it'll come to the same, I will never see her again. It is one of those self-dramatizing loves, like a bullfighter lifting his hat towards a beshawled lady and dropping it in the sand at her feet, that only has meaning for her and me. It's incredible to me how fourteen-year-olds manage to keep their clothes on, how they restrain their hormones from leaping out and devastating the land.

I knew José-Ramón would not come: I have to go through this alone now. At 6.45 am I pay for my drinks and slowly make my way out of the bar. I move to the left, she moves to the left. I move to the right, she moves to the right. I say '*Perdón, señorita.*' It is the shortest conversation I've ever had with a lover. We don't know each other's names. I brush past her. She turns her back to me, shows me her neck as a way of preserving and giving herself at the same time.

I stand in the spot I stood with José-Ramón the first morning. I am running with the bulls like a coward today, scared shitless. This isn't right. You don't run out of duty, alone, stone cold sober. You run with friends, full of sunlight and oaths and champagne.

I still see José-Ramón holding me, that first morning we met, telling me that you have to be eighteen to run, that the police will arrest me if I dare break loose and go on my own. We are at the barrier, and he is sweating, biting down on his cigarette, letting the smoke enter his eyes, so his hands are free to squeeze both my wrists.

'Now swear to me, you little bastard, that you won't run.'

'I swear it.'

'If you run I will never speak to you again, so help me God. You are only thirteen, a snotnose, and I will break your rotten ass if you try anything smart.'

The first *cohete* explodes. José-Ramón is looking up and down the street. 'I gave Maruja my word, so I don't want you to make a liar out of me.'

I wait for the second *cohete*, wait for the rumbling of hooves on the cobblestones. José-Ramón trusts me and is not suspecting anything, he is waiting for the bulls to appear. Promises and pie crusts are meant to be broken. I turn, yank my arm out of his and sprint up the street.

He shouts my name. '*Niño!*'

He is racing after me. But he is drunk and out of breath, and already a mass of runners separates us. He has a look in his face of utter helplessness.

'*Niño, por Dios*, don't do this to me, you wise-ass shit!'

I don't turn my head again. I don't dare slow down or

stop. I keep running like hell. Scared of the bulls and terrified of what José-Ramón will do to me when he catches up with me again.

We meet in the bullring. José-Ramón wants to slap me, but instead he squeezes my arms until he stops the flow of blood, lifts me off the ground and shakes me hard, baring his yellow nicotine-stained teeth. The skin of his face has the lustre and transparence of Scotch tape. His sweat drips on my face, and he keeps shaking me. 'You shit, you fucking shit, don't you ever do that to me ever again!'

During breakfast at a café terrace, he recounts my first run to everyone he meets. He is proud of me. After that, we run together every morning. Of course, we lie to Maruja.

This year, running alone, I don't make it into the bullring, and it's just as well, my heart isn't in it.

On the last day of the fiesta, when everyone is throwing themselves flat on the ground, singing '*Pobre de mi*' ('Poor me, poor me, the fiesta is over'), Teresa goes home. Or perhaps Uncle Alfonso yanks her out of my grip sooner, because what was meant to last a week feels like a few hours. When I see her off at the Pamplona train station, I am overcome with sadness. I tell her, '*Te quiero mucho.*' In Spanish it sounds better than in English because it means both, I like you, and I love you. I promise I will see her soon again, but I never do. I don't see any of my cousins until two decades later.

*

In my mid thirties I find myself in Madrid on an assignment to write about 'The new Spain', and the only cousin in town is Short María. She is married to a physics engineer who now works as a florist. As we walk one evening she says, 'The problem with growing up here is that the men make the women carry all the honour of Spain.'

'They load your backs like Ludivino, the donkey?'

'It's not on our back we carry it. It's between our legs.'

I stay quiet, unused to this post-Franco directness.

'Joaquín wanted his daughters to be virgins for ever. The boys were encouraged to go out and bed anything that moved. I suppose proof was needed that they were not homos – the great Spanish *macho* phobia. But we girls were supposed to be saints. I hated my youth.'

Maybe that is what I saw that day under the table, searching for my fork – not Tall María, but the Honour of Castile and maybe that is what came between us.

CHAPTER SEVENTEEN

The last train

'Maruja is dead.'

When I hear this over the telephone, I am alone in my kitchen in Washington DC preparing dinner, and I have trouble believing it. I am in graduate school and have just turned twenty-two.

'What did she die of?' I ask my mother.

'Cancer.'

'I didn't know she was sick.'

'It happened several months ago,' says my mother. 'But I only just heard of it now.'

I hang up in shock. For a while I refuse to believe she is gone. I have lost touch with her for several years, and this call both recreates her in my mind and takes her away. I regret not talking to her, not seeing her one last time. But I've been spared the spectacle of her disease, so I have the luxury of remembering her always healthy (except for her nervous attacks), always full of laughter and sunlight.

How quickly life stops after death! If she had to die, I would have preferred a slow fade. In movies I always like seeing the ship captain's hat floating on the surface of the ocean after his boat sinks.

I feel small and empty without Maruja. She is my first close loved one to die. I keep remembering the last time I saw her in Paris, when Maruja tried to teach me how to cook. She basted a chicken and put it in the oven. I was bored with these mechanics, but I loved watching her repeating the same gestures I had seen her do countless times. Slicing open those big fat Mediterranean tomatoes, those sweet Spanish onions, drowning them in olive oil, and eating with a soup spoon to get the maximum of vinaigrette. I was sixteen, but she still spoonfed me.

I never understood what Maruja found so great about growing old, it seemed to me like a waste of time.

'No, really, *niño*, if I could have any wish in the world, anything at all, you know what I would want? To grow old with Manolo, just the two of us.' She bends over laughing. 'I can see Manolo and me walking down an avenue together – him with a cane, and me with grey hair, hanging on to his arm. It would be so sweet – like two old dogs.'

Now her words strike me as sad and prophetic. I put her out of my mind. I want to deny her death, forget it, soar above it. I avoid asking details, avoid writing to Manolo or her family. When *Saturday Night Live* makes fun of Franco, quoting the ageing fossilized dictator who is in a coma as saying, 'I am still not dead yet,' I switch off the TV in disgust.

Yet over the years friends tell me about her last days. She had a virulent stomach cancer that spread in spite of all the chemo and radiation they tried on her. She was operated on in Paris, but the doctor sewed her up without doing anything. That is when she decided to return for the last time to Galicia and be with her family. She knew she was dying and wanted to be back with Cariño, to put her house in order, see her family and say goodbye to her daughter.

'Can you imagine what a bastard Manolo was,' says my mother. 'Maruja asked to fly home, but rather than spend the extra two hundred bucks on a plane ticket to Vigo, he sent her by train.'

'Yes, but they went first-class.'

'She could hardly walk, hardly sit down. What a bastard, just to save a little money!'

I imagine Maruja on her last train ride home. I am with her, sitting across from her. She is leaning back in her seat like an overweight gouty monarch who can't sit up straight. She keeps staring out of the window in order not to miss the border. Although this is a carbon copy of dozens of trips she has taken, the fact that it is her last makes it unlike any other, and she knows it. At Saint-Jean-de-Luz already tears start flowing down her fat round cheeks, rounder now because of the cortisone. She wipes her cheeks off with her palm. Some tears blossom on her white blouse.

I enter her compartment to share her last voyage. We

are travelling off-season, and we have the compartment to ourselves. There are no suitcases crowding the first-class hallway, no soldiers blowing cigarette smoke in our face, no stench of hard-boiled eggs, oranges or *chorizo* sandwiches. It's so civilized here, the white headrest cloth is newly pressed, the cushions clean, the air smells of lavender wax, we are quite alone – it's almost as if the other passengers know.

Before the train comes to a full stop at Hendaye, Maruja is already standing. Her limbs have swollen up, so that Manolo has ripped all her pant legs and blouse arms to be able to dress her, and she has a perfect excuse to be the Barefoot Contessa. She waddles past the French customs officials, shoes in hand. Manolo opens the two carry-on bags, one full of medicine, the other with some Swiss chocolate and Colombian coffee, but the guard waves us through without even standing up. She is such a walking disaster that people rush out of her way. Manolo holds her elbow to steady her, but she no longer sees him or bothers scolding him.

I clatter-clatter down steps, rushing after her. She has done this border crossing so many times, she could do it blind, but today the Irún death-dash has a more literal meaning.

Pell-mell through an underpass. Up steps. Waving tickets at a conductor who holds his whistle in his mouth, holding it in abeyance while the last stragglers climb aboard the Spanish Talgo. Maruja lurches towards a first-class door. A dozen passengers with suitcases are crowding into second-class. Because this is Spain and not France, no one bothers stowing the bags into the overhead carriers. We leave ours in the hallway, blocking the way.

Maruja is thrilled to chat with her countrymen. It is as if her round bloated body were chock-a-block with nostalgia looking for escape. While chatting to a priest she asks Manolo to massage her feet. She tells them about Cariño, how *traviesa* she is in school, how the nuns are at their wits' end with her, how bossy and independent she is. How Cariño refuses to take exams, how she draws with indelible ink on doors and walls and clothes. She talks about Cariño the same incessant way she used to talk about me. And if Cariño were here, passengers would stare at her, and she would blush the way I used to blush. And no doubt the child would politely suggest that Maruja shut up, but on this last trip there is no chance of reining her in. Anyway Cariño isn't here, she is only in Maruja's mind.

I can't recall ever having seen Maruja take a nap. All her life she woke early and worked and drank coffee until late at night. But now, with the drugs they have prescribed, she naps all the time. When she wakes up, she orders coffee black with three sugars. I light a menthol Cool for her.

Maruja sits in her first-class compartment, hands folded over her wide girth, chest rising and falling, and she partakes of her last guilty pleasure. She blows out the smoke without inhaling and is blessedly quiet for a while.

I keep seeing us visiting Ronalda, sitting in the hinterland drizzle. She too died of cancer. So did their mother. I tell Maruja about her sister Josefa's scrotal handshake, but she waves me away and closes her eyes.

Every so often she opens her eyes and stares at the distant sea, like a snoozing cat who is just checking that everything is OK. She no longer has that eager expectancy she had in France. A few times she calls out the names of towns we pass without opening her eyes: Donostia, San Sebastián, Tolosa, Beasain, Zumárraga, Altsasu.

'*Niño*, marry a Spanish girl. They are so much more *salada*. They are the saltiest girls in the world. You will never find any one better.'

There's no good translation for what a Spaniard means when he says a girl is 'salty'; it means she is witty or spunky, but a woman's saltiness can also often drive a man crazy. Maruja uses it to mean everything a man wants to but cannot control in a woman. Except for the connotation of cute, Maruja is the most *salada* woman I know.

Manolo is holding her feet in his lap, massaging them. Her cheeks are burning bright red.

Alsasua, Gasteiz, Vitoria, Miranda de Ebro, Briviesca, Burgos, Venta de Baños, Palencia.

'Tell me, *niño*, tell me again about that woman you met on the plane going to New York.'

She closes her eyes and smiles as I describe how I was on a transatlantic flight and an old Jewish lady from New Jersey sitting next to me started crying. I asked her if she was all right, and she said that the previous year her

205

husband, who had a weak heart and cancer, had died in flight, and rather than alert the crew and make the plane return to Paris where the authorities would have taken the body away from her, she held him in her arms the whole way to New York. It happened during the movie, she said, and she just held her husband for three hours, keeping him warm, kissing his forehead. Only after the plane landed did she tell a flight attendant and let them take him away.

'*Que bonito*,' Maruja whispers.

I am watching Manolo massaging the soles of Maruja's feet that for forty-two years have carried an impossible load. The way I see it, he is the one who needs to be carried, not she, he is the one who is being abandoned here.

'Cariño is only seven, I left her with my sister Josefa because I did not want her to see me all swollen. Now she will be shocked by my appearance. She will know.'

Maruja laughs recalling Lolli, the baby duck she bought for her daughter. Lolli has many times been saved from Josefa's stewpot and now follows Cariño everywhere she goes.

León, Veguellina, Astorga, Bembibre, Ponferrada, O Barco de Valdeorras, A Rúa-Petín, San Clodio-Quiroga.

Maruja is staring at the blue of the blue sea, and the long day is waning. The sunset reminds me of all the fireworks she and I watched together, all the reds and blues that shot downward with such speed and majesty we thought they would cascade right into our eyes and burn us. The colours this evening are too red, too dramatic. I never liked those golden Turners. All my life I found them too ornate, too overdone, then I saw a Turner exhibit at the Grand Palais and began understanding him.

Some years later, going through a lot of family junk in the basement, throwing away old files, I find the French social security payment stubs and receipts for Maruja's many years of working for us. I find the two-wheeled stand-up shopping cart she used to use. I even locate the small wine cask with copper goblets I won at Pamplona's fair. After earning the points to win it and taking it home, I never once played with it or looked at it again. Though a packrat, someone who adopts every stone my son brings me and keeps them in my pockets for months, I throw out all these mementoes of Maruja. They are better conserved in my mind.

I get a telephone call from Aunt Conchita. Uncle Joaquín is dead, and she is calling my mother with the news. Though frail and in her eighties, Conchita tells me, 'Maruja was fantastic, fantastic, she was a miracle of generosity, loyalty and goodness. I have never met anyone so fantastic. She was life itself.'

Conchita, thinner than ever, with her endless rosary beads and holy water, is so direct, so exact, saying words I always felt but never had the courage to voice, that I put down the phone elated, feeling far stronger and wiser than when I picked it up.

Monforte de Lemos, Ourense, Ribadavia, Frieira, Salvaterra. Maruja's last twenty-four-hour train ride takes for ever. It is a trip through her memories and her soul. Past Guillarei, O Porriño, Redondela, never quite reaching Vigo. RENFE trains go so slowly that even the blue Talgo express stops in the countryside for no reason.

I keep remembering one tiny incident. At one unscheduled stop in the middle of nowhere – Maruja claimed a boy had stuck his head out of the window and been decapitated in a tunnel, but with hindsight I suspect that was to keep us from leaning out – a girl in her early twenties leaps off and runs to pick a sunflower from a big yellow field about a hundred metres away. Everyone in the train watches her run, thinking the same thought.

'She won't make it,' whispers Maruja.

The more she runs, the further the field recedes. Then she disappears among the sunflowers for what seems like ages.

The entire time that the girl takes to catch up with our stalled train, Maruja keeps whispering, 'You'll make it, come on baby, you'll make it, child. That's it, don't lose heart.'

But now I see the girl running back towards us through sunlight, running with three round sunflowers she has picked, is Maruja. I can hear her unmistakable high-pitched laugh preceding her. One hand is holding those impossibly large breasts of hers which weigh so much she has to take pills to alleviate the strain. The other hand is clamping her straw sunhat down on her head.

The train snorts and shakes. And Maruja keeps coming, full of flowers, laughter and sunlight.

CHAPTER EIGHTEEN

Concerning love

Years go by, and although I often wonder about Manolo's fate, I am unable to get in touch with him.

Through the grapevine I hear that Cariño has turned into a hellion. (Maruja always liked that about her: 'She's a troublemaker, good, that means she will get somewhere in life.') Cariño has got kicked out of three schools in a row for smoking cigarettes, for letting boys into her room, and for running away. I cannot imagine how gentle Manolo is coping with her.

Every time I ask my mother to help me locate him, she calls him 'that bastard' and repeats how he made Maruja take the train instead of flying her home. I defend Manolo, mention his gentleness, and that no doubt Maruja's death has devastated him. But neither my mother, nor anyone who knew them both, thinks much of Manolo. Did they never understand him?

'He was shy.'

'He was a dumb cluck,' insists my mother.

'He was always a prince to me.'

'She had all the charm, all the brains in that family. Manolo was a nothing. Just cruel. And by the way, he is ruining that adopted daughter of theirs.'

'The Manolo I know would never hurt a fly. He was as loyal as they come.'

Some ten years after Maruja dies, I am in Paris, and my mother manages to locate him quite by accident. In the middle of the conversation, she says, 'I understand Manolo is going through a big life change.'

'What do you mean?'

'Well, let him tell you about that.'

'Has he remarried?'

'They say he is a homosexual.'

'Oh, come on!'

'That's what I hear.'

I start to laugh.

'He lives with a man. You ask him.'

Manolo is working for a count again, another French count. I am nervous about meeting him, feeling guilty that I never wrote to him after Maruja's death, never called him, never sent a telegram or a card, but back then I didn't know how important these were.

He appears at our door, his V-Wilson knot perfectly tied, wearing a blue blazer, looking as handsome as the evenings when he used to wait on fancy dinner parties. His hairline has retreated several centimetres up his forehead to the crown of his head, but otherwise his hair looks exactly the same. Perhaps more dignified, more respectable, but that same goofy half-smile of his gives him away.

Manolo must be dyeing his hair, because his eyebrows are grey, almost white. He still walks duckfooted, with his overlapping toes and corns buckling up the ends of his shoes, his pants ride low on his hips. His face and delicate clean hands are as white as ever, his fingernails perfectly buffed.

I am thirty-two now and he is in his mid sixties, but it feels as if we never lost sight of each other. He could be taking me to school again in a city bus. Sensing my mother's resentment, he sits uncomfortable on the edge of his chair waiting for me to talk. But even after she leaves us alone in the apartment, Manolo remains timid.

When he answers me monosyllabically, he whispers. I realize how many of the myths and crazy stories he told me were built on his long silences.

Manolo, who never drank anything but wine, asks for a Scotch. We discuss old times. He talks a lot about his daughter.

'The Mother Superior called me in and told me Cariño was a whore. She said she never knew any child so wretched. It seems Cariño instigates illegal parties. She gets boys to jump over the wall, and she hides them in the convent school on weekend nights. Mother Superior asked me what I was going to do. She asked me how I raised her? Did I discipline her? I shrugged. I said my influence is limited. Mother Superior asked me if I was ashamed of myself?' Manolo smiles naughtily. 'Cariño is sixteen. She likes to smoke and fuck boys. Nothing wrong with that, is there?'

We talk all evening.

At one point, even though I know it may embarrass him, I can't help myself, I touch his white soft cheek that smells of cologne. 'It's good to see you again, Manolo, really good.'

I am again the boy under the sheets, farting and hugging them both, one arm around Manolo's neck skinny and perfumy, another around Maruja's neck which is not a neck at all but the place where head and shoulders meet. I hug them both to me very hard.

They laugh. '*Aie, aie, aie, aie, aie, aie. Deja me, deja me, no me toques, no, no, nnnooooooooooooooooooooooooooooooooooo!*'

Manolo divulges nothing about his current living arrangements. He walks through our apartment, remembering how when he and Maruja made the master bed and found the sheets soiled, they would know my parents were back on good terms together.

Knowing I may never see him again and this may be my last opportunity, I ask, 'Is it true you are living with a man?'

He turns beet red.

'You can tell me, Manolo. I don't care if you are homosexual. What is his name? What nationality? Come on, Manolo, everyone knows. Why hide it? Is he American? German?'

After a silence, 'He's French.'

'Is he old? I mean older than you?'

'He's my age.'

'What does he do?'

Another silence. Manolo looks around the room to see if there is anyone else in the apartment.

'He is a butler like me.'

'Can I see his picture?'

'I don't carry any pictures.'

'Manolo, are you, you know ... sort of, well, *mariquita*?'

He nods.

I try not to embarrass him, not to laugh. We smile.

'Weren't you happy with Maruja?'

'Never.'

'No, come on, tell me the truth. I know you were happy. In spite of all the fights and the arguments, she loved you more than anything in the world.'

'I wasn't happy.'

'You're saying that now, but I saw you two happy as loons and full of love for each other.'

'Maruja was demanding, difficult, bossy, and crazy.'

'No, for once in your life tell me the truth.'

'I am telling you the truth.'

Manolo never talked freely to adults, never talked to them at all if he could avoid it, never felt at ease with them. When I was an adolescent we were equals; now, without wanting it, I am talking from a position of superiority.

'What is it like? I mean sex with your lover?'

'Great.'

No, seriously, tell me.'

'Love-making is great – stronger than with a woman. He is courteous. He never shouts at me.' Manolo smiles to himself. 'I am telling you the truth. It is easier living with a man than with a woman. Try it, you will never go back.'

'But were you always . . . I mean when you were living with Maruja were you . . . interested in men?'

'I don't know.'

'Well, how did you find out?'

Manolo does not give a straight answer. He may not know himself, or does not want to tell me.

At the end of the evening I offer to drive him home. He declines, saying there is a direct metro. But we have talked past 1 am, and the metro is closed. Manolo accepts my offer of a ride. I have never seen him drink like this before, but because he is always pulling practical jokes and stunts, I assume when he stumbles and slips to the ground that he is faking it, or exaggerating his drunkenness.

In the car, as I drive him, Manolo tells me he is not certain where he lives or what his phone number is. Twenty times Manolo takes me in the wrong direction. He keeps telling me to drop him off on any corner, that he will make it home on foot. But I don't want Manolo stumbling about drunk in the middle of the night, I don't want to drop him off any old place.

At first our driving in circles is funny, but after a while

it becomes frustrating. It strikes me that he may not want me to see where he lives or have his address.

'Manolo, if you don't want me to know where you live, just tell me, and I swear that as soon as I drop you off I will forget your address for ever. I'll respect your privacy.'

'OK, leave me here.'

'Is this near where you live?'

'No.'

'You don't want me to know, is that it?'

'Yes.'

'Why, don't you trust me?'

'It's here.'

'Is it really here?'

'Yes, this is where I live, number 76, you can watch me go up the stairs if you like.'

We're both tired. We kiss on the cheeks. I watch him close the door and fumble with his keys. He can't handle liquor like he used to, but he never had much capacity. I don't write down his address and don't save his telephone number.

I have never gotten in touch with him since, because that was my implicit promise to him. And now I have lost track of him.

I keep hoping I will bump into him again.

I have a three-year-old son. And often when I put him to bed and try to get him to sleep at night, he asks me, '*Porqué me quieres?*'

It's a simple question: why do you love me? Everything I tell him he asks *porqué?*, so it is only natural he should question why I love him. At first I tell him, 'I love you because you are a good boy.' But as he keeps asking me the same question over and over, I am forced to think of new answers: I love you because you give me lots of kisses, because you are an angel, because *tu eres un angelito de Dios*. It is a question I never asked myself before. I always assumed that 'Do you love me?' was far more important.

My son could be a bad boy, he could be ugly, naughty, the worst boy in the history of mankind, and I would not love him any less. Why do we love those we love? My son has an answer. He keeps telling me, 'I love you because you love me.'

For months his question stumps me. *Porqué me quieres?* Then I am at the Père Lachaise cemetery for the funeral of a friend's father. It is a rather social affair, with a lot of Parisian and expatriate ladies wearing stylish broad-brimmed black hats and men in dark suits shaking hands and signing the guestbook. During the ceremony that precedes the cremation, there is a short eulogy for the deceased, and I hear the speaker ask, 'Why do you love me?' It happens so seldom at a funeral full of dusty words that one runs across anything relevant to one's life, that I sit up. The man at the lectern is saying: 'Like Oedipus before the Sphinx we want the answer to what we can never know. Why do you love me? It is the most important question one can ask, and one that can never be answered.

Because if we answer it, if we define it, we kill it. So we discuss only where or how we met, what we did together. That is as close as we can come to knowing the essence of our love.'

I see that is what I have been doing in writing this for Maruja and Manolo. Like a fly going around and around a single point, I have never landed on the central issue, I have avoided the heart of the matter. I have described the furniture in the room, the dust filling the shafts of bright sunlight, the sound of her cooking, the smell of her lush sizzling olive oil, her seafood *paellas*. And maybe it is enough that I am the fly buzzing around this room where Maruja and Manolo invited me. I wanted to give them back their voice.

The centre can to a limited extent be described by its boundaries. But maybe the scenery, the staging, the acting is all part and parcel of the unknowable centre, so that what I have described here is not at all ancillary or incidental but necessary, and because it cannot be separated from the love, in a way it defines it and becomes it.

To love is to allow yourself to be haunted. We discover this only after a person dies, and then the haunting becomes central, but maybe it always was central, and we simply were too busy, too distracted to realize it.

Paris, January–June 1994